NICHOLAS COUNTY

KENTUCKY

PROPERTY TAX LISTS

1800–1811

with Indexes to
Deed Books A & B (2), and C

Carrie Eldridge

HERITAGE BOOKS
2015

HERITAGE BOOKS

AN IMPRINT OF HERITAGE BOOKS, INC.

Books, CDs, and more—Worldwide

For our listing of thousands of titles see our website
at
www.HeritageBooks.com

Published 2015 by
HERITAGE BOOKS, INC.
Publishing Division
5810 Ruatan Street
Berwyn Heights, Md. 20740

International Standard Book Numbers
Paperbound: 978-1-58549-938-0
Clothbound: 978-0-7884-6117-0

TABLE OF CONTENTS

INTRODUCTION

Tax lists are an excellent research aid often overlooked by researchers. Although many states have enacted laws allowing them to destroy old tax lists, many lists from the Nineteenth Century have been microfilmed and are available from several sources. Most Kentucky tax lists exist from the founding of each county until 1890.

Tax lists aid in two important ways. First, they show you who was present in the county at the time the tax was assessed, and second, they provide a comparison for name spelling. Most of the lists are done by alphabetical section. Although not in order, all the A's are listed together followed by the B's, etc. This is helpful if you have names like Lee and See for example. One exception is found under I & J. Most frontier clerks combined these letters into one heading.

The first section of the book shows information gathered for four different tax years. They show not every tax assessor asked the same questions nor was each clerk careful in spelling and recording. This first section lists streams where the properties were located, thus helping a researcher place his settler in a certain section of the county. It also shows who first claimed the property or provided surety, which type of land was taxed and how much the property was worth.

One mistake many researchers commit is looking at just one year of records. The second section of this books compares the tax records for eleven years. This study shows various name spelling changes, numerous sons, hidden settlers and poor record keeping. Eleven years was selected because it covered two census period. Although the 1800 census was reconstructed from the 1800 tax list, the 1810 tax list shows additional settlers not enumerated by the census and persons "passing through" perhaps recorded by the census taker when they could be stopped in the county. This happened because Nicholas County was on the major trail between Cumberland Gap, the Kentucky Bluegrass and the Ohio River.

The third section shows an expanded census for 1810 while the fourth section offers the deed book indexes of the period for name comparison.

Nicholas County is located in the north central portion of Kentucky directly north of Lexington. It is bisected by US 68, formerly known as the Limestone/Lexington Pike. (Limestone is now called Maysville.) The road led from central Kentucky to the Ohio River and was a favored route in the late Eighteenth Century. It was such an important road that it actually received federal money for construction in the early Nineteenth Century.

Nicholas County is much smaller than originally laid out. Robertson County and a portion of Fleming County where both taken from the northern section of old Nicholas County. Other smaller areas have also gone to various surrounding counties. Your settler might have later records in another county.

The original tax lists listed owner, amount of property, tax rate of a-b-c land value, who entered the land, who had it surveyed and who patented the property. Entry, survey and patent could have been several persons and not necessarily the taxed person. Some information had to be excluded to save space.

ent/sur = entered/surveyed - tax payer was not necessarily person who entered the land or had it surveyed.

NICHOLAS COUNTY, KY
TAX LISTS

(1) voters　　　　　(3) slaves
(2) white males　　(4) horses

N-sd = North side　　a-rd = above road
S-sd = South side　　b-rd = below road

Year	Person	Location & Water Course	ent/sur	(1) voters	(2) W MALE	(3) slaves	(4) horses	stud
1800	Ardery, James	a-rd	Brushey Fork	1	1		3	
1800	Adams, William	a-rd	-West	1	1		2	
1800	Archer, John	a-rd		3	4		4	
1800	Anderson, James	a-rd		1	1		4	
1800	Adams, Thomas	a-rd		1	1		3	
1800	Allen, William	a-rd	Sommerset -L.Fowler	1			5	
1800	Adams, Ralph	a-rd		1				
1800	Anderson, George	a-rd		1	2		3	
1800	Arnott, Samuel		Brushey Fork -Garnet	1	1	2	2	
1800	Allison, John	N-sd		1	1	2	2	
1800	Anderson, John	N-sd	Elk Creek	1	2		2	
1800	Ashcraft, Jacob	N-sd		1	1		2	
1800	Art, William	N-sd		1	2		2	
1800	Allison, Alexander	N-sd		1	1			
1800	Atkins, John	N-sd		1	1			
1800	Arnold, H. Lewis	N-sd		1	1		1	
1800	Byers, David	a-rd	Brushey Fork -Halens	1	1		2	
1800	Benson, James	a-rd		1	2		3	
1800	Bell, Robert	a-rd	Brushey Fork -Fleming -B.Pendleton	1	1		3	
1800	Bowen, William	a-rd		1	1		1	
1800	Boatman, Henry	a-rd		1	2		4	
1800	Brown, James	a-rd		1	1		4	
1800	Beard, John	a-rd	Brushey Fork	1	1			
1800	Berry, Robert	a-rd	Sommerset -L. Fowler	1	1	1	4	
1800	Benson, John	a-rd		1	1		1	
1800	Bell, John	a-rd		1	1	1	3	
1800	Bennington, Nehemiah		Brushey Fork -Stockden	1	1		2	
1800	Benton, William	a-rd	Brushey Fork -Halens	1	1		3	
1800	Benton, John	a-rd	Brushey Fork	1	1		1	

Year	Person	Location & Water Course		ent/sur	(1)	(2)	(3)	(4)
1800	Beard, John	a-rd	Brushey Fork		1	1		
1800	Bailey, John	a-rd			1	1		
1800	Burwell, Ephraim	a-rd	Brushey Fork	-Fleming	1			2
1800	Blair, Alexander	a-rd	Sommerset	-Fowler/Black	1	1	1	4
1800	Bell, Adam	a-rd	Lees Creek		1	1		5
1800	Beard, William	a-rd			1			
1800	Boyd, William	a-rd	Sommersett	-Abercrommy	1	1	1	2
1800	Boyd, John	a-rd		-Abercrommy	1	1	1	4
1800	Benton, James	a-rd		-Fowler	1	1		3
1800	Baker, Martin	b-rd	Hinkson		1	1	2	8
1800	Barnet, Ambross	b-rd	Brushey Fork	-Garnet	1	1		8
1800	Brown, John	b-rd	Willmers Run	-A. Moor	1	1		3
1800	Barlow, William	b-rd		-Cook	1	1	1	2
1800	Barlow, John	b-rd			1	1		1
1800	Burden, James	b-rd	Hinkson	-Rice	1	2		2
1800	Baker, William	b-rd		-Rice	1	1	5	4
1800	Burden, John	b-rd			1	1		
1800	Buckner, Robert	b-rd	Panther Creek	-Clater	1	1	40	12
1800	Barlow, Thomas	a-rd	Willmers Run	-Cook	1	1		2
1800	Basket, Jesse	a-rd	Hinkson	-Kees	1	1	2	2
1800	Baker, Martin, Jr.	a-rd		-Ragsdale	1	2	7	5
1800	Black, Richard	a-rd				1		
1800	Baker, James	a-rd			1	1	1	1
1800	Buchannan, James	N-sd			1	1		1
1800	Bolen, William	N-sd	Cedar Creek	- Kenton	1	1		1
1800	Ballingall, David	N-sd	Johnston	-A.Thornton	1	1	1	2
1800	Bentley, Michael	N-sd	Tates Creek		1	1		3
1800	Brinson, Thomas	N-sd			1	1		3
1800	Bartlett, William	N-sd			1	1		5
1800	Bartlett, Ebenzer	N-sd			1	1		1
1800	Bartlett, Samuel	N-sd			1	1		1
1800	Bedinger, M. George	N-sd	Licking	- E.Powel	3	3	14	21
1800	Brinson, Jonathan	N-sd	Kentucky		1	1		
1800	Boon, Abner	N-sd			1	1		
1800	Boon, Jacob	N-sd			1	1		1
1800	Blackburn, William	b-rd	Indian Creek		1	1		2
1800	Berry, John	b-rd		- Minter	1	1		3
1800	Buckner, Phillip	b-rd			1	1		1
1800	Crawford, Samuel	a-rd	Brushey Fork	-Myars	1	2		3
1800	Campble, William	a-rd	Stepstone	-Campble	1	1		6
1800	Craig, Margaret	a-rd						3

Year	Person	Location & Water Course	ent/sur	(1)	(2)	(3)	(4)
1800	Clemmons, John	a-rd	Stepstone		1	1		2
1800	Craig, John	a-rd	Stepstone			1		
1800	Craig, James	a-rd				2		
1800	Caldwell, David	b-rd	Sommerset	-Fowler	1	1		4
1800	Campble, Jossias	b-rd			1	1		8
1800	Caldwell, Robert	b-rd			1	1		3
1800	Caldwell, William	b-rd	Sommerset		1	1		4
1800	Campble, William	b-rd	Sommerset		1	1		
1800	Caldwell, William	b-rd			1			1
1800	Caldwell, Alexander	b-rd	Sommerset		1	1		6
1800	Caldwell, Robert, Jr.	b-rd			1	1		1
1800	Caldwell, David	b-rd	Sommerset		1	1		
1800	Cassidy, Daniel	a-rd	Sommerset	-Gates	1	3		3
1800	Cowan, Issac	a-rd	Cassidy		1	2		4
1800	Chipman, Drake	a-rd	Cassidy		1	1		1
1800	Campble, James	a-rd			1	1		1
1800	Clark, John	a-rd			1	1		3
1800	Cowan, John	a-rd	Brushey Fork	-Halems	1	1		1
1800	Casey, James	a-rd			1	1		2
1800	Crab, Bazel	b-rd			1	1		
1800	Conway, John	b-rd	Hinkson	- Conway	1	1	2	4
1800	Cottrel, Thomas	b-rd		- Rice	1	1		3
1800	Coyle, John	b-rd			1	1		2
1800	Carbough, Jacob	b-rd	Indian Creek	-Harison	1	1		1
1800	Carothers, Thomas	b-rd	Indian Creek	-Young	1	1		4
1800	Collier, John	b-rd	Hinkson	- Barksdale	1	1	25	13
1800	Collier, A. Coleman	b-rd			1	1		
1800	Collier, Hamlet	N-sd			1	1		
1800	Caughey, John	N-sd			1	1		
1800	Campble, James	N-sd	Johnston	- Throckm'rtn	1	1		4
1800	Campble, David	N-sd	Johnston		1	1		
1800	Cameron, John	N-sd			1	1		
1800	Catherwood, Charles	N-sd	Cedar Creek	- Kenton	1	1		1
1800	Cotter, David	N-sd	Cedar Creek	- Kenton	1	1		1
1800	Catherwood, Samuel	N-sd	Cedar Creek	- Kenton	1	1		2
1800	Cameron, Samuel	N-sd	Cedar Creek	- Kenton	1	1		2
1800	Cameron, John	N-sd			1	1		
1800	Clark, Solomon	N-sd			1	1		
1800	Carver, (no name)	N-sd			1	1		
1800	Corwine, George	N-sd			1	1		
1800	Davidson, John	a-rd	Sommerset		1	1		(3)

3

Year	Person	Location & Water Course		ent/sur	(1)	(2)	(3)	(4)
1800	Dalton, Garret	a-rd	Sommerset		1	1		
1800	Dinsmer, Samuel	a-rd	Brushey Fork	- Myars	1	1		7
1800	Darland, Isaac	a-rd			1	1		
1800	Deal, Mathew	a-rd			1	1	1	1
1800	Dinsmer, Henry	a-rd			1	1		4
1800	Downey, Arch.	a-rd			1	1		2
1800	Davidson, Thomas	a-rd			1	1		5
1800	Dinsmer, John	a-rd	Brushey Fork	- Berry	1	1		4
1800	Dils, Isaac	a-rd	Indian Creek		1	1		4
1800	Drumins, James	b-rd	Hinkson	- Rasdale	1	1		2
1800	Davis, Levi	b-rd			1			
1800	Duvall, Martin	b-rd			1	1	4	2
1800	Dils, Abraham	b-rd	Hinkson	- Crawford	1	1		2
1800	Davis, Eli	b-rd			1	1		
1800	Dansson, Henry	N-sd	Johnston	-(Davsson)	1	1		4
1800	Dailey, Bryan	N-sd	Beaver	- Kenten	1	2	2	1
1800	Davis, Philemon	N-sd			1			
1800	Davis, Robert	N-sd			1	1		
1800	Duzan, Jacob	N-sd	Buchannon	- Moseby	1	2		5
1800	Drake, John	N-sd			1	1	1	1
1800	Eubanks, James	a-rd			1	1		1
1800	Ellis, James	a-rd	Money Creek		1	1		6
1800	Easley, John	a-rd	Cassiday	- Franklin	1	1		4
1800	Easten, Phillip	a-rd			1	1		1
1800	Earlywine, Daniel	b-rd			1	1		5
1800	Earlywine, George	b-rd	Wilmore R.		1	2		3
1800	Enlow, Jesse	b-rd			1	1	1	3
1800	Easly, Francis	b-rd	Beaver	- " & Young	1	1		3
1800	Eavans, Walter	b-rd			1	1		2
1800	Ellis, John	N-sd			1	1		1
1800	Foreman, John	a-rd			1			
1800	Forkner, George	a-rd			1	1		1
1800	Fryer, Robert	a-rd			1			
1800	Ferren, Hugh	a-rd			1	1		2
1800	Frazer, James	a-rd			1	1		1
1800	Frazer, George	a-rd			1	1		5
1800	Frakes, Benjamin	a-rd			1			
1800	Forsyth, John	a-rd			1	1		2
1800	Forsyth, Jenny	a-rd				1		7
1800	Fearman, John	b-rd			1	1		
1800	Fite, Gilbert	b-rd			1			

Year	Person	Location & Water Course	ent/sur	(1)	(2)	(3)	(4)
1800	Fite, John	b-rd	Beaver		1			
1800	Foster, Thomas	b-rd			1			
1800	Fields, Benjamin	b-rd			1	1		2
1800	Fields, (no name)	b-rd			1	1		2
1800	Fryman, Phillip	a-rd	Beaver	- Evans	1	1		2
1800	Frazer, William	a-rd						
1800	Fanbs, James	N-sd			1	1		2
1800	Gamble, David	a-rd	Licking		1	1		2
1800	Gray, Joseph	a-rd			1	1		1
1800	Gray, Anny	a-rd				1		2
1800	Glassgow, James	a-rd			1			1
1800	Gray, David	a-rd	Somerset	- Leach/Fowler	1	1		3
1800	Gidions, John	b-rd			1	1		1
1800	Galbreath, Andrew	b-rd			1	1		
1800	Galbreath, Benjamin	b-rd	Licking	- Bell	1	1		4
1800	Galbreath, John	b-rd			1	1		
1800	Gidions, James	b-rd			1	1		1
1800	Glasscock, Daniel	b-rd			1	1		3
1800	Glasscock, Daniel	b-rd			1	1		3
1800	Gidions, Henry	b-rd			1	1		5
1800	Goehegan, John	b-rd			1	1		4
1800	Galbreath, William	b-rd			1	1		4
1800	Gonce, Nicholas	b-rd	Hinkton	- Rice	1			1
1800	Gonce, George	b-rd			1	1		
1800	Griffin, Gabriel	b-rd			1	1		1
1800	Grossowmer, Richard	b-rd			1	1		
1800	Glasscock, Samuel	b-rd	Licking		1	1	1	5
1800	Gowsnel, William	N-sd	Ekin Creek		1	1		1
1800	Guften, Amos	N-sd			1	1		1
1800	Gray, David	N-sd			1	1	2	2
1800	Gattinel, Thomas	N-sd			1			
1800	Hugh, William	N-sd			1	1		5
1800	Hamilton, John	N-sd			1	1		5
1800	Hamilton, Abd.	N-sd			1	1		3
1800	Hamilton, Robert	N-sd			1	1		
1800	Hamilton, James, Jr.	N-sd		- Myans	1	1		2
1800	Hamilton, Elias	a-rd			1	1		1
1800	Hanna, Samuel	a-rd	Somerset	- Fowler	1	1		2
1800	Hill, James	a-rd			1	1		1
1800	Hall, Benjamin	a-rd	Somerset/Johnston - Laird		1	3		4
1800	Hall, Cornelius	a-rd	Somerset	- Abercromby	1	1	5	4

Year	Person	Location & Water Course	ent/sur	(1)	(2)	(3)	(4)	
1800	Hamilton, Samuel	a-rd			1	1			
1800	Hall, Moses	a-rd	Brushey Fork	- Fleming	1	1	1	3	
1800	Hixson, Benjamin	N-sd			1	1		3	
1800	Hall, James	a-rd	Somerset	- Fowler	1	2	9	7	
1800	Hariston, John	a-rd			1	1			
1800	Harmesson, Wallace	a-rd			1	1		3	
1800	Harmen, Robert	a-rd			1	1			
1800	Howard. Gidion	a-rd		- Abercromby	2	3			
1800	Hawkins, Thomas	a-rd			1				
1800	Hill, John	a-rd			1	1		5	
1800	Holladay, William	b-rd	Brushey Fork	-Garnet	1	1	2	4	
1800	Helpman, John	b-rd	Wilmers Run	- Young	1				
1800	Harney, Mills	b-rd			1	2		2	
1800	Harney, Hiram	b-rd			1	1			
1800	Harney, Rollen	b-rd			1	1		1	
1800	Hofman, Peter	b-rd	Wilmers Run	- Rice	1	1		4	
1800	Hart, Zepheniah	N-sd			1	2			
1800	Howard, Mary	N-sd			1	2		2	
1800	Harden, Elihu	N-sd	Licking	- T.A. Bens	1	1	1	2	
1800	Hall, Thomas	N-sd	Cedar Creek	- Kenten	1	1		1	
1800	Hunter, John	N-sd			1	1			
1800	Hyson, Jacob	N-sd			1	1		2	
1800	Hawkins, Samuel	N-sd	Licking	- T.C. Owings	1	1	1	2	
1800	Hildreth, Squire	N-sd	Licking	- T. Martain	1	1		3	
1800	Harison, Garrett	N-sd			1	1			
1800	Irvin, David	a-rd			1	1		3	
1800	Jolly, David	a-rd			1	1		7	
1800	Johnston, John Jr.	a-rd	Brushey Fork	- Myans	1			3	
1800	Johnston, John Sr.	a-rd			1	1		1	
1800	Johnston, Lewis	a-rd				1		1	
1800	Jones, John	a-rd			1	1		2	
1800	Jones, Thomas	a-rd							
1800	Jenins, Solomon	a-rd			1	1		1	
1800	Jones, Jacob	b-rd			1	2		4	
1800	Johnston, Jonathan	b-rd	(Wihiuno----)	- Clater	1	1			
1800	Jorden, William	b-rd			1	1			
1800	Jones, Moses	b-rd			1	1	2	4	
1800	Jones, John, Jr.	b-rd			1	1	7	6	
1800	Johnston, Major	b-rd			2	2		2	
1800	Johnston, James	b-rd	Indian Creek	- Young	1	1		3	
1800	Jones, Jacob	N-sd	Indian Creek		1	1		4	

Year	Person	Location & Water Course	ent/sur	(1)	(2)	(3)	(4)	
1800	Jones, William	N-sd		1	1		1	
1800	Johnston, James	N-sd		1	1		1	
1800	Jones, Jacob	N-sd	Ceder Creek	- Kenten	1	1	1	2	
1800	Jones, William	N-sd	Johnston	- Thornton	1	1	1	2	
1800	Jinkins, Samuel	N-sd	Licking	- Powell	1	2		3	
1800	Kennedy, Andrew	a-rd			1	1		1	
1800	Kincart, Samuel	a-rd	Brushey Fork	- Fleming	1	1		5	
1800	Killgore, William	a-rd			1	1			
1800	Kinten, Phillip	b-rd	Licking		1	1		5	
			Fleming	- Allison					
1800	Kenedy, David	b-rd	Willmers Run	- A. Moor	1			1	
1800	Kimbro, Samuel	b-rd			1	1		1	
1800	Kimbro, Richard	b-rd	Hinkson	- Rasdale	1	1			
1800	Kimbro, John	b-rd			1	1	12	5	
1800	Keith, Jacob	N-sd			1				
1800	Kays, John	N-sd	Johnston		1	1		2	tl
1800	Kentt, John	N-sd			1	1		1	
1800	Keith, Phillip	N-sd	Ceder Creek	- Kenten	1	1		2	
1800	Loughridge, John	a-rd	Sommerset	- Fowler	2	3		8	
1800	Loughridge, William	a-rd			1	1		2	
1800	Leeper, John	a-rd			1	1	5	8	
1800	Leeper, William	a-rd			1	1		2	
1800	Long, Benjamin	b-rd			1	1	3		
1800	Lilly, Pleasant	b-rd			1	1		1	
1800	Lilly, Anieger	b-rd	Hinkson	- Reece	1	1	1	3	
1800	Lars, George	b-rd	Indian Creek	- Young	1	1		1	
1800	Leavengood, George	b-rd			1	1			
1800	Leach, Benjamin	N-sd			1	1		1	
1800	Louderback, Andrew	N-sd			1	1		1	
1800	Leonard, Michael	N-sd			1				
1800	Leonard, Valentine	N-sd	Ceder Creek	- Kenten	1	1		4	
1800	Livingston, David	N-sd			1	1		1	
1800	Lee, George	N-sd			1	1			
1800	Loan, Isaac	N-sd			1	1		1	
1800	McCune, Robert	a-rd			1	1		3	
1800	McCune, John	a-rd			1	1		2	
1800	Mathers, Samuel	a-rd			1				
1800	McPherren, James	a-rd			1	1		1	
1800	Mitchel, William	a-rd	Brushey Fork	- Shull	1	1		4	
1800	Mitchel, James	a-rd			1	1		1	
1800	Morgan, John	a-rd	Brushey Fork	- Fleming	1	1			

Year	Person	Location & Water Course		ent/sur	(1)	(2)	(3)	(4)	
1800	Morgan, Rece	a-rd		- Myans	1	1		2	
1800	Morgan, David	a-rd			1	1		3	
1800	McGriff, Richard	a-rd			1	1		1	
1800	McFerren, William	a-rd			1	1			
1800	McFerren, Samuel	a-rd			1	1		2	
1800	Monhollen, Patrick	a-rd			1			3	
1800	Matlock, Samuel	a-rd			1	1		1	
1800	Mitchel, John	a-rd		- Stockden	1	1		4	
1800	Marshall, (Arch) ?	a-rd	Licking	- W. Bell	1	1	2	5	
1800	McCormach, James	a-rd	Brushey Fork	- T. West	1	3		4	
1800	Morgan, Garret	a-rd			1	1		2	
1800	Moore, Samuel	a-rd			1	1	2	1	
1800	Martain, John	a-rd			1	1		2	
1800	McInutty, Joseph	a-rd	Somerset	- Fowler	1	1		3	
1800	McIntire, Andrew	a-rd		- Fowler	1	1		2	
1800	Mathers, William	a-rd	Brushey Fork	- Stockden	1	1		3	
1800	Marsh, Thomas	a-rd		- Bolard & Prt	1	1	6	4	
1800	Marshall, David	a-rd			1	1			
1800	Myers, George	a-rd	Cassidy	- Young	1	2		3	
1800	Myers, John	a-rd			1	1		3	
1800	McClannahan, James	a-rd			1	1		1	
1800	McClannahan, Wm.	a-rd			1	1		1	
1800	McDonald, Joseph	a-rd			1	1		3	
1800	McDonald, George	a-rd			1	1		3	
1800	Morris, Thomas	a-rd			1	1			
1800	McMahan, Robert	a-rd	Sommerset	- Halems	1	1	3	4	
1800	Murphey, H. George	b-rd			1	1		3	
1800	McKee, James	b-rd			1	1		2	
1800	McDonald, Mordicay	b-rd			1	1		2	
1800	Mitcheltree, (Jesse)	b-rd			1	1			
1800	Megines, William	b-rd			1	1			
1800	McDonal, Alexander	b-rd			1	1			
1800	McIntire, Robert	b-rd	Wilmers Run	- Cook	1	1	1	4	
1800	McClintock, Hugh	b-rd	Hinkson	- H. Thomspn	1	1		1	
1800	McClintock, Joseph	b-rd		- H. Thompsn	1			5	
1800	Menteen, Robert	b-rd			1	1		1	
1800	McCotten, John	b-rd			1	1		1	
1800	Menteen, John	b-rd			1	1		1	
1800	McCracken, John	b-rd		- Young	1	1	1	2	
1800	McShan, Sarah	b-rd			1	1			
1800	Miller, Abraham	b-rd	Indian Creek	- Young	1	1			

Year	Person	Location & Water Course		ent/sur	(1)	(2)	(3)	(4)
1800	McFarland, William	b-rd		- Young	1	1		2
1800	Marshall, Ralph	b-rd	Beaver		1	2		2
1800	Marshall, Samuel	b-rd			1	1		1
1800	McDonald, Alexander	b-rd	(single man)			1		
1800	Man, John	b-rd	Brushey Fork	- Ingrams	1	1		1
1800	Man, George	b-rd		- Ingrams	2	3		4
1800	Man, Jacob	b-rd		- Ingrams	1	1		3
1800	McDonald, William	b-rd	Wilmers Run		1	1		
1800	McCarty, David, Jr.	b-rd			1	1		
1800	McCormick, James	b-rd		- Young	1	1		2
1800	Morgan, Joseph	N-sd			1	1		
1800	McCord, William	N-sd			1	1		
1800	McCord, Michael	N-sd			1	1		
1800	Metcalf, Eli	N-sd	Johnston	- Walden	1	1	5	2
1800	McCord, David	N-sd			1	1		
1800	McCord, Wm., Sr.	N-sd			1	1		1
1800	McClurgh, Joseph	N-sd	Elk Creek		1	1		2
1800	McCarty, David	N-sd			1	3		2
1800	Mitchel, Robert	N-sd			1	1		
1800	(Morton, Throck), John "		Johnston	- Throckmrtn	1	1	5	4
1800	Metcalf, Rhodey	N-sd	Ceder Creek	- J. Metcalf				1
1800	Metcalf, Thomas	N-sd		- J. Metcalf	1	1		
1800	Mason, Burgess	N-sd			1	3	2	3
1800	Martain, Zedehiah	N-sd			1	1		1
1800	McCracken, John	N-sd			1	1		4
1800	Miller, William	N-sd			1	1		1
1800	McCormick, John	N-sd			1	1		
1800	Morgan, Charles	N-sd			1	1		
1800	Martain, John	N-sd	Johnston	- Johnston	1	1		4
1800	Morris, Jacob	N-sd		- Kenten	1	1		1
1800	McClintock, Joseph, Jr. "		Ceder Creek	- Kenten	1	1		1
1800	Nesbet, Thomas	a-rd	Brushey Fork	- Fleming	1	1		4
1800	Nickel, Robert	a-rd			1	1		
1800	Nesbet, Nathan	a-rd		- Fleming	1	1		5
1800	Newcum, Daniel	a-rd			1	1		1
1800	Nicholas, John	N-sd			1	1		
1800	Nudigate, William	N-sd	Johnston	- Thornton	1	2		3
1800	Oden, William	N-sd			1	1	2	1
1800	Oliver, John	N-sd	Ceder Creek	- Kenten	1	1		3
1800	Parks, James	a-rd	Brushey Fork	- Fleming	1	1		3
1800	Palmer, Robert	a-rd	Brushey Fork	- Shull	1	1	1	1

Year	Person	Location & Water Course		ent/sur	(1)	(2)	(3)	(4)	
1800	Peyton, Stephen	a-rd		- S. Noble	1	2		2	
1800	Peyton, William	a-rd			1				
1800	Peyton, Samuel	a-rd			1	1			
1800	Porter, William	a-rd			1	1			
1800	Paxton, Robert	a-rd			1	1		3	
1800	Pumel, Every	a-rd			1	1			
1800	Plue, Philip	a-rd			1	1			
1800	Potts, William	a-rd	Somerset	- Fowler	1	1	4	4	
1800	Peyton, Thomas	a-rd			1	1		1	
1800	Price, John	a-rd			1	1		1	
1800	Powel, Thomas	a-rd		- Abercrumy	2	3		15	1
1800	Polley, John	a-rd		- Coxes	3	3		3	
1800	Plue, Elias	a-rd		- Fowler	1	2		1	
1800	Plue, Jemimah	a-rd		- Fowler	1	1		2	
1800	Paugh, Henry	a-rd			1	1		2	
1800	Parks, Robert	b-rd			1	1		4	
1800	Pumel, William	b-rd			1	1		4	
1800	Porter, Thomas	b-rd			1	1		1	
1800	Porter, John	b-rd			1	1		1	
1800	Phillip, Michal	b-rd			1	1		1	
1800	Pritchet, William	N-sd	Licking	- Henry	1	1	2	1	
1800	Perren, C. W.	N-sd			1	1	1		
1800	Pursley, William	N-sd			1	1			
1800	Rachford, Robert	a-rd			1	1			
1800	Riddel, William	a-rd	Brushey Fork	- Halims	1	1			
1800	Robertson, Richard	a-rd			1	1			
1800	Razor, Henry	a-rd			1	1		1	
1800	Ray, James	a-rd			1			6	
1800	Ray, Frances	a-rd		- Stockden	1	1		3	
1800	Reviel, Thomas	a-rd			1	1		1	
1800	Robertson, Samuel	a-rd			1			3	
1800	Roberts, Henly	a-rd	Somerset	- Fowler	1	1		2	
1800	Roberts, (Uriah)	a-rd			1	1		2	
1800	Richey, Robert	a-rd	Willmers Run	- Cook	1	1		2	
1800	Reily, John	a-rd	Somerset	- Fowler	1	1		6	
1800	Rhoads, Becham	a-rd	Licking	- Cassdy	1	1		2	
1800	Roberts, Thomas	a-rd			1	1			
1800	Robertson, James	a-rd	Brushey Fork	- Halims	1	1	1	4	
1800	Reviel, Joseph	a-rd	Cassidy	- Cassiday	1	1		1	
1800	Reed, William	a-rd	Brushey Fork	- Halims	1	3		3	
1800	Richey, Gilbert	b-rd	Brushey Fork		1	1		2	

Year	Person	Location & Water Course		ent/sur	(1)	(2)	(3)	(4)	
1800	Rubey, Joseph	b-rd	Indian Creek		1	1		2	
1800	Richey, Isaac	b-rd			1	1		1	
1800	Roase, Abraham	N-sd			2	2	1	5	
1800	Ray, Samuel	N-sd			1	1		1	
1800	Sanderson, John	a-rd	Licking		2	2		2	
1800	Sanderson, John, Jr.	a-rd			1	1		2	
1800	Shields, William	a-rd			1	1		4	
1800	Smart, Joseph	a-rd			1	1		2	
1800	Scott, Adam	a-rd			1				
1800	Scott, Thomas	a-rd			1	1			
1800	Sample, Robert	a-rd			1	1		1	
1800	Stephenson, James	a-rd	Somerset	- Fowler	1	1		3	
1800	Stephenson, William	a-rd			1	1		3	
1800	Stephenson, Robert	a-rd			1	1		1	
1800	(Stoops), Phillip	a-rd	Licking	-Gates/Cassidy	1	1		2	
1800	Shankland, John	a-rd	Cassdy	-Gates/Cassidy	1	1	1	2	
1800	Sparks, Joseph	a-rd			1	1		1	
1800	Sanders, James	a-rd	Somerset	- Fowler	1	1		3	
1800	Shannon, Thomas	a-rd		- Fowler	1	1		2	
1800	Shaw, John	a-rd			1			1	
1800	Shillinger, Adam	b-rd	Brushey Fork	- Ingram	1	1		4	
1800	Shaw, William	b-rd			1	1		1	
1800	S---der, John (ink)	b-rd	Willmers Run	- Cook	1	1			
1800	Sumet, Christopher	b-rd	Hinkson		1	1		6	
1800	Snap, Peter	b-rd			1	1		4	
1800	Snap, George	b-rd			1				
1800	Stewart, Robert	b-rd				1			
1800	Sumet, George	b-rd			1	1		4	
1800	Stewart, John	b-rd		- Rasdale	1			3	
1800	Stephenson, Thomas	b-rd		- Young	1	1		4	
1800	Stephenson, (Havers)	b-rd	Indian Creek	- Stephenson	1	1	6	6	
1800	Stewart, Joseph	b-rd		- Young	1	1		2	
1800	Stubs, Anny	b-rd		- Crawford			3	6	
1800	Scott, John	b-rd		- Young	1	1		1	
1800	Scott, Gabriel	b-rd			1				
1800	Scott, Mathew	b-rd			1	1		4	
1800	Scott, Moses	b-rd			1	1		1	
1800	Scott, Thomas	b-rd			1	1		1	
1800	Sandiford, Nathan	N-sd			1	1	5	8	tav
1800	Swarts, James	N-sd			1	1		4	
1800	Stewart, Mathes	N-sd	Indian Creek		1	1			

Year	Person	Location & Water Course	ent/sur	(1)	(2)	(3)	(4)	
1800	Smith, John	N-sd		1	1		2	
1800	Shaw, Henry	N-sd		1	1		1	
1800	Sworden, Quinten	N-sd		1	1		2	
1800	Scott, Solomon	N-sd	Johnston	- Harison	1	1		2	
1800	Stewart, Williby	N-sd		1	1		1	
1800	Shively, John	N-sd		1	2			
1800	Stewart, James	N-sd		1	1			
1800	Smith, William	N-sd		1	1		1	
1800	Standiford, Elijah	N-sd		1	1		1	
1800	Standiford, Aquila	N-sd		1	1			
1800	Sanders, Fitzhugh	N-sd	- Johnston	1	1		1	
1800	Tate, Francis	a-rd		1				
1800	Thompson, Joseph	a-rd		1	1	2	1	
1800	Tanner, James	a-rd		2	1			
1800	Toppins, Robert	a-rd		1	1			
1800	Thompson, James, Jr.	a-rd	Somerset	- Fowler	2	1		7	
1800	Thompson, Anthony	a-rd		1				
1800	Thompson, Alex.	a-rd		1	1		2	
1800	Thompson, William	a-rd		1	1		7	
1800	Thomas, Edward	b-rd	Wilmers Run	- A. Moor	1	1		1	
1800	Thompson, Henry	b-rd	Hinkson	- M. Thompsn	1	2		9	
1800	Thompson, Thomas	b-rd		1	1		2	
1800	Trousdale, William	b-rd		1	1			
1800	Trousdale, John	b-rd	Indian Creek	- Young	1	1		1	
1800	Taylor, William	b-rd		1	1		1	
1800	(Tully), John	b-rd		1	1		1	
1800	Taylor, William	b-rd		1	1		2	
1800	Taylor, Thomas	b-rd		1	1		1	
1800	Taylor, James	b-rd	Ceder Creek	- Kenten	1	1		1	
1800	Taylor, Thomas	b-rd		1	1		1	
1800	Taylor, Leason John	b-rd		1	1			
1800	Willson, Benjamin	a-rd		1	2		2	
1800	Waugh, Samuel	a-rd	Brushey Creek - West		1	1	1	4	
1800	Wills, John	a-rd		1	1		1	
1800	Williams, John	a-rd	Somerset	- Fowler	1	1		1	
1800	West, Isaac	a-rd	Cassidy	- Cassidy	1	1		3	
1800	Wood, John	a-rd		1	1		2	
1800	Wishard, William	a-rd		1	1		1	
1800	West, Amos	a-rd		1	1	5	3	
1800	Wiley, John	a-rd		1	1			
1800	Wiley, Samuel	a-rd	Locust(Fleming Co.)		1	1			

Year	Person	Location & Water Course		ent/sur	(1)	(2)	(3)	(4)	
1800	Wisely, William	a-rd			1	1		2	
1800	Waugh, George	a-rd			1	1			
1800	Waggoner, Christian	a-rd	Bever Creek		1	1		2	
1800	Williams, Hubbard	a-rd			1	1	9	2	
1800	Webb, Anny	a-rd	Hinkson	- Young	1	1		1	
1800	Webb, William	a-rd			1	1			
1800	Waits, John	a-rd	Indian Creek	- Young	1	1		2	
1800	Waggoner, John	a-rd	Beaver		1	1		2	
1800	Wheeler, William	a-rd			1	1			
1800	Ward, Thomas	N-sd			1	1			
1800	Wallace, William	N-sd	Johnston	- Johnston	1	1		3	
1800	Welch, Abraham	N-sd			1	1	1	9	
1800	Wolf, Joseph	N-sd			1	1	1	4	
1800	Weaver, William	N-sd			1	1		4	
1800	Wiggons, John	N-sd		- Johnston	1	1		5	
1800	West, Thomas	N-sd		- Johnston	1	1		2	
1800	Ward, Andrew	N-sd		- Harison	1	1		1	
1800	Ward, George	N-sd		- Harison	1	1		1	
1800	Watson, James	N-sd	Licking	- Kinten	2	3		2	
1800	Wilson, Benjamin	N-sd			1	1		4	
1800	McDowell, William		Brushey Fork	- A. Noble	1	1		2	
1800	Vaughn, Daniel		Johnston		1	1			
1800	Vennoy, Francis			-Montgomery	1	2	1	2	
1800	Vaughn, Thomas				1	1	6	9	
1800	Young, William				1				
1800	Young, Jacob				1	1		5	

Male inhabitants   503
White Tithebles   512
Slaves over 16   119
Total slaves   248
Horses   1059
Stud horse   4
Tavern License   2
One town lot
Presented by Commissioner James Parks
Nicholas County, KY - 1800
Received by Lewis H. Arnold 4th November 1800

LET COMMON SENSE BE YOUR GUIDE

In 1800 there was a very limited number of given names. They varied pertaining to region, but once you catch the pattern it is much easier to read the names. It seems there is almost always an odd name with many repeats. Probably a very early settler who was influential or Grandpap and his 14 sons.

Common to this region of Kentucky:
Mainly Biblical - Scot-Irish with a few Germans and one or two English.

#1	#2	#3	#4
David	Alexander	Andrew	Charles
James	Benjamin	Henry	Edward
John	George	Jeremiah	Jesse
Isaac	Jacob	Jonathan	Moses
Thomas	Robert	Joseph	Solomon
William	Samuel	Jossiah	Zachariah
		Joshua	

The old hand writing is difficult, but keeping in mind the limited number of name options helps to choose your spellings. The clerks used many abbreviations, but the only one that really causes trouble is Jas./Jos. because you can never decide if it's an "a" or an "o". Luckly Jos. was only Joseph with most clerks. With this list you will not make mistakes like Alex. when the "x" looks like an "n". Allen was used, but not common while Alenn would appear in the 20th Century. Your name is Alexander, just abbreviated. Have you ever read an "R" that looked like and "N" because the clerk was lazy? There are thousands of Roberts, few Norberts. Try to learn the clerks writing quirks. It will help in the long run.

German? Christian not Christopher - If you just use printed materials, you have little concept of missed interpertations. Go to the original.

The choice of given names in an area will indicate what group settled. Predominance of Peter, Jacob, Christain and William - German.
Edward, Edmund, Allen - English

14

NICHOLAS TAX LIST 1801

Year	Person	Location & Water Course		ent/sur	(1)	(2)	(3)	(4)	s
1801	Adams, William	a-rd		-West	1	1		3	
1801	Archer, John	a-rd	Brushey Fork		3	4		7	
1801	Ardery, James	a-rd	Brushey Fork		1	1	1	6	
1801	Abner, William	a-rd	Somerset	- Fowler	1			6	
1801	Anderson, James	a-rd			1	1		3	
1801	Allen, William	a-rd	Sommerset	-L.Fowler	1	1			
1801	Anderson, George	a-rd			1	2		3	
1801	Adams, Ralph	a-rd			1			1	
1801	Adams, Thomas	a-rd			1	1		2	
1801	Arnott, Samuel	b-rd			1	1	2	2	
1801	Allen, James	b-rd			1	1		1	
1801	Arnold, H. Lewis	N-sd			1	1		1	
1801	Allison, John	N-sd	Johnston	- B.L. Harison	1	1		3	
1801	Allison, Alexander	N-sd			1	1			
1801	Ashcraft, Jacob	N-sd			1	1		4	
1801	Anderson, John	N-sd	Ceeder Creek		1	1		1	
1801	Art, William	N-sd			1	2		3	
1801	Art, Robert	N-sd			1	1			
1801	Art, William, Jr.	N-sd			1	1		1	
1801	Bell, Robert	a-rd	Brushey Fork	-Fleming	1	1	1	3	
1801	Brown, David	a-rd			1	1			
1801	Byers, David	a-rd	Brushey Fork	-Halens	1	1		2	
1801	Bennington, Nehemiah	"	Brushey Fork	-Stockden	1	1		3	
1801	Bell, John	a-rd			1	1		3	
1801	Beard, John	a-rd	Brushey Fork		1	1		2	
1801	Brown, James	a-rd			1	1		2	
1801	Benton, James	a-rd	Somerset	-Fowler	1	1		5	
1801	Beard, George	a-rd			1	1		3	
1801	Boatman, Henry	a-rd			1	1		3	
1801	Boatman, William	a-rd			1	1		1	
1801	Benton, John	a-rd	Somerset		1	1		1	
1801	Benson, James	a-rd			1	2		2	
1801	Bailey, John	a-rd			1	1		1	
1801	Bell, William	a-rd			1	1			
1801	Benson, John	a-rd			1	1		2	
1801	Beard, John	a-rd			1	1		1	
1801	Benton, William	a-rd	Somerset	-Halens	1	1		1	

Year	Person	Location & Water Course		ent/sur	(1)	(2)	(3)	(4)
1801	Boyd, William	a-rd		- Abercromy	1	1	1	3
1801	Boyd, John	a-rd		-Abercrommy	1	1		5
1801	Bright, Hanson	a-rd	Somerset		1	1		3
1801	Blair, Alexander	a-rd	Sommerset	-Fowler/Black	1	1	1	13
1801	Brown, John	b-rd	Willmers Run	-A. Moor	1	1		3
1801	Barlow, John	b-rd			1	1		1
1801	Barlow, William	b-rd		-Cook	1	1	1	3
1801	Barlow, Thomas	b-rd	Willmers Run	-Cook	1	1		3
1801	Burden, Benjamin	b-rd			1	1		
1801	Baker, William	b-rd	Hinkson	-Rice	1	1	4	2
1801	Baker, Martin	b-rd	Hinkson		2	2	8	3
1801	Baker, James	b-rd			1	1	4	2
1801	Burden, James	b-rd	Hinkson	-Rice	1	1		2
1801	Burden, John	b-rd			1	1		
1801	Blackburn, William	b-rd	Hinkson	- Young	1	1		3
1801	Barnet, Ambross	b-rd	Brushey Fork	-Garnet	1	1		4
1801	Basket, Jesse	b-rd	Hinkson	-Rece	1	1	1	2
1801	Bosby, William	b-rd			1	1		
1801	Buckner, Robert	b-rd	Brushey Fork	- Howe	1	2	34	15
1801	Bolen, William	N-sd	Cedar Creek	- Kenton	1	1		1
1801	Bailey, Basel	N-sd			1			
1801	Boon, Abner	N-sd			1	1		
1801	Ballingall, David	N-sd	Johnston	-A. Thornton	1	1		2
1801	Buchannan, James	N-sd			1	1	1	6
1801	Brinson, Thomas	N-sd			1	1		3
1801	Bartlett, William	N-sd	Licking	- Young	1	1		2
1801	Bartlett, Ebenzer	N-sd			1	1		1
1801	Bartlett, Samuel	N-sd			1	1		1
1801	Barnet, James	N-sd			1			
1801	Bentley, Michael	N-sd			1	1		2
1801	Bedinger, M. George	N-sd	Licking	- E.Powel	1	1	14	19
1801	Craig, James	a-rd				1		
1801	Cowan, John	a-rd	Brushey Fork	-Halems	1	1		1
1801	Carpoell, Edward P.	a-rd			1	1		
1801	Craig, John	a-rd			1	1		3
1801	Caldwell, Robert	a-rd	Somerset	-Fowler	1	1		4
1801	Crawford, Samuel	a-rd	Brushey Fork	-Myars	2	2		3
1801	Cassady, James	a-rd			1	1		
1801	Chipman, Draper	a-rd	Cassidy		1	1		1
1801	Collier, Coleman	a-rd			1	1		1
1801	Campble, Jossias	a-rd	Somerset		1	1		8

16

Year	Person	Location & Water Course		ent/sur	(1)	(2)	(3)	(4)
1801	Caldwell, William	a-rd	Sommerset		1	1		4
1801	Caldwell, David	b-rd	Sommerset		1	1		8
1801	Caldwell, Robert	a-rd			1	1		2
1801	Cassidy, Daniel	a-rd	Sommerset	-Gates	2	3		2
1801	Cowan, Issac	a-rd	Cassidy		1	1		3
1801	Caldwell, David	a-rd	Sommerset	-Fowler	1	1		
1801	Caldwell, Alexander	a-rd	Sommerset		1	1		6
1801	Crawford, John	a-rd			1	1		
1801	Campbel, James	a-rd			1	1		2
1801	Caldwell, William	a-rd			1			2
1801	Campbel, William	a-rd	Sommerset		1	1		
1801	Carter, Jonathan	a-rd	Licking		1	2		2
1801	Conway, John	b-rd	Hinkson	- Conway	1	1	2	4
1801	Carbough, Jacob	b-rd	Indian Creek	-Harison	1	1		3
1801	Carothers, Thomas	b-rd	Indian Creek	-Young	1	1		5
1801	Collier, John	b-rd	Steels Run	- Barksdale	2	3	20	11
1801	Coyle, John	b-rd			1	1		2
1801	Collins, John	b-rd			1			
1801	Crab, Bazel	b-rd			1	1		
1801	Campbel, David	N-sd	Johnston		1	1		4
1801	Caughy, John	N-sd			1	1		1
1801	Campbel, James	N-sd	Johnston	- Throckm'rtn	1	1		4
1801	Cameron, Samuel	N-sd	Cedar Creek	- Kenton	1	1		1
1801	Cameron, John	N-sd			1	1		
1801	Cotter, David	N-sd	Cedar Creek	- Kenton	1	1		
1801	Catherwood, Charles	N-sd	Cedar Creek	- Kenton	1	1		1
1801	Davidson, John	a-rd	Somerset	- Halims	1	1		4
1801	Dinsmer, John	a-rd	Brushey Fork	- Berry	1	1		3
1801	Darland, Isaac	a-rd			1	1		
1801	Dinsmer, Henry	a-rd			1	1		4
1801	Dinsmer, Samuel	a-rd	Brushey Fork	- Myars	1	1		7
1801	Deal, Mathew	a-rd			1	1	2	1
1801	Davidson, Thomas	a-rd			1	1		4
1801	Downey, Arch.	a-rd			1	1		2
1801	Dalton, Garret	a-rd	Sommerset		1	1		
1801	Dils, Isaac	a-rd	Indian Creek		1	1	1	3
1801	Davis, Eli	b-rd			1	1		2
1801	Drumins, James	b-rd	Hinkson	- Rasdale	1	1		2
1801	Dils, Abraham	b-rd	Indian Creek	- Crawford	1	1		3
1801	Davis, Levi	b-rd			1	1		1
1801	Davis, Robert	N-sd	Beaver		1	1		1

Year	Person	Location & Water Course		ent/sur	(1)	(2)	(3)	(4)
1801	Dailey, Bryan	N-sd	Ceeder Creek	- Kenten	1	1	2	3
1801	Dailey, S. John	N-sd			1	1		
1801	Dunkon, Joseph	N-sd	Licking		1	3	7	4
1801	Davison, Henry	N-sd		-(Davsson)	1	1		5
1801	Duzan, Jacob	N-sd	Buchannon	- Moseby	1	2		3
1801	Drake, John	N-sd	Licking		1	1	5	2
1801	Eubanks, James	a-rd			1	1		2
1801	Edmuston, Moses	a-rd			1	1		
1801	Easley, John	a-rd	Cassiday	- Franklin	1	1		4
1801	Ellis, James	a-rd			1	1		
1801	Earlywine, George	b-rd	Wilmore R.		1	2		3
1801	Easely, Joseph	b-rd			1	1		2
1801	Eavans, Walter	b-rd			1	1		2
1801	Earlywine, Daniel	b-rd			1	1		4
1801	Easly, Francis	b-rd	Beaver	- " & Young	1	1		4
1801	Enlow, Jesse	b-rd			1	1	1	2
1801	Ellis, John	N-sd			1	1		1
1801	Fields, Ebenzer	N-sd			1	1		4
1801	Forsyth, Jean	N-sd			1	2		7
1801	Forsyth, John	N-sd			1	1		2
1801	Frazer, James	N-sd	(Fleming Co.)		1	1		1
1801	Fisher, Alexander	N-sd			1	1		
1801	Foreman, John	N-sd			1			
1801	Foster, Robert	N-sd			1	1		
1801	Fryman, Robert	N-sd			1			
1801	Foster, Thomas	b-rd			1			2
1801	Fryman, George	b-rd			1	1		1
1801	Fite, John	b-rd			1	1		1
1801	Fields, Thomas	b-rd			1	1		2
1801	Fryman, Phillip	b-rd	Beaver	- Evans	1	1	1	1
1801	Frazer, William	b-rd			1			1
1801	Frazer, William, Jr.	b-rd			1			
1801	Fields, James	N-sd			1	1		2
1801	Fields, Benjamin	N-sd			1			
1801	Fearman, John	b-rd			1	1		
1801	Givens, James	a-rd	Beaver		1	1		1
1801	Gibsen, Thomas	a-rd			1	1		2
1801	Gray, David	a-rd	Somerset	- Leach/Fowler	1	1		2
1801	Gray, James	a-rd			1	1		1
1801	Gamble, David	a-rd	Licking		1	2		2
1801	Glassgow, James	a-rd			1			2

Year	Person	Location & Water Course	ent/sur	(1)	(2)	(3)	(4)	
1801	Gidions, John	b-rd		1	1		1	
1801	Gray, Ann	a-rd		1	1		3	
1801	Gray, Joseph	a-rd		1	1		2	
1801	Gidions, Henry	b-rd	Wilmers Run - Haws	1	1		3	
1801	Gidions, James	b-rd		1	1			
1801	Goehegan, John	b-rd		1	1		6	
1801	Gray, Robert	b-rd		1				
1801	Gonce, George	b-rd		1	1			
1801	Gonce, Nicholas	b-rd	Wilmers Run - Kennedy	1			2	
1801	Griffith, Joseph	b-rd		1	1	3	2	
1801	Griffin, Gabriel	b-rd		1	1		1	
1801	Garnet, Philip K.	b-rd	(Barren Co.)	1	1	2	4	
1801	Galbreath, William	b-rd		1	1		3	
1801	Grossowmer, Richard	b-rd		1	1			
1801	Galbreath, Benjamin	b-rd	Licking - Bell	1	1		2	
1801	Galbreath, John	b-rd		1	1			
1801	Glasscock, Samuel	b-rd	Licking	1	1	3		
1801	Gray, David	N-sd	Johnston	1	1	3	3	
1801	Gattirel, Thomas	N-sd	Ceeder	1	1		1	
1801	Glasscock, Daniel	b-rd		1	1		4	
1801	Gonslen, William	N-sd		1	1		2	
1801	Hall, Moses	a-rd	Brushey Fork - Fleming	1	1	1	3	
1801	Hamilton, James, Jr.	a-rd	- Myans	1	1		2	
1801	Hall, James	a-rd	Somerset - Fowler	1	2	6	4	
1801	Housten, John	a-rd		1	2			
1801	Hamilton, Elias	a-rd		1	1			
1801	Hughs, William	a-rd		1	2			
1801	Hamilton, Samuel	a-rd		1	1			
1801	Hamilton, John	a-rd	McCords Creek -Sturgus	1	1		5	
1801	Hamilton, Abad.	a-rd		1	1		4	
1801	Hill, John	a-rd		1	1		5	
1801	Hill, James	a-rd		1	1		3	
1801	Hawkins, Thomas	a-rd		1	1		3	tav
1801	Hall, Benjamin	a-rd	Somerset/Johnston - Low	1	3		4	
1801	Hall, Cornelius	a-rd	Somerset - Abercromby	1	1	4	4	
1801	Hamilton --	a-rd	Somerset	1	1		3	
1801	Harmen, Robert	a-rd		1	1		1	
1801	Harison, Garrett	a-rd		1	1			
1801	Hanna, Samuel	a-rd	Somerset - Fowler	1	1		3	
1801	Holladay, William	b-rd	Brushey Fork -Garnet	1	1	3		1 s
1801	Hofman, Peter	b-rd	Wilmers Run - Rice	1	1		5	

Year	Person	Location & Water Course		ent/sur	(1)	(2)	(3)	(4)	
1801	Helpman, John	b-rd	Hinkson	- Young	1			2	
1801	Harney, Hiram	b-rd			1	1			
1801	Harney, Rolen	b-rd			1	1		2	
1801	Harney, Mills	b-rd			1			1	
1801	Howard, Jacob	N-sd			1	1		1	
1801	Hisler, William	N-sd			1	2			
1801	Howard, Mary	N-sd			1	3		1	
1801	Hall, Thomas	N-sd	Cedar Creek	- Kenten	1	1		2	
1801	Harden, Elihu	N-sd	Licking	- T.A. Bens	1			4	
1801	Harden, James	N-sd			1	1			
1801	Harlen, Moses	N-sd			1	1			
1801	Hunter, John	N-sd			1	1			
1801	Hizer, Jacob	N-sd			1	1		2	
1801	Hawkins, Samuel	N-sd	Licking	- T.C. Owings	1	1	1	2	
1801	Hildridge, Squire	N-sd	Licking	- T. Martain	1	1		2	
1801	Ishmal, Benjamin	a-rd	Brushey Fork		1				
1801	Irvin, David	N-sd	Ceeder Creek	- Kinten	1	1	1	1	
1801	Johnston, Lewis	a-rd	Licking		1	1		1	
1801	Johnston, John	a-rd	Brushey Fork	- Myans	1			4	
1801	Johnston, Isham	a-rd			1	1	1	2	
1801	Jones, John	a-rd			1	1		2	
1801	Jones, Thomas	a-rd							
1801	Jolly, David	a-rd			1	1		5	
1801	Johnston, Arthur	a-rd			1	1			
1801	Johnston, John Sr.	a-rd			1	1		1	
1801	Jorden, William	a-rd			1	1			
1801	Johnston, Jonathan	b-rd	Wilmers Run		1	1			
1801	Jones, Moses	b-rd			1	1	2	4	
1801	Jones, John, Jr.	b-rd	HInkson		1	1	6	5	
1801	Johnston, Major	b-rd	Indian Creek		2	2		1	
1801	Jones, Jacob	b-rd			1	2		5	
1801	Jinkins, Samuel	N-sd	Licking	- Powell	1	2		4	
1801	Jones, Jacob	N-sd	Indian Creek		1	1	1	1	
1801	Jones, William	N-sd	Johnston	-Thornton	1	1	4	1	
1801	Kincart, Samuel	a-rd	Brushey Fork	- Fleming	1	2		4	1s
1801	Keaseg, James	a-rd	Brushey Fork		1	1		2	
1801	Killgore, William	a-rd			1	1		2	
1801	Killgore, Olliver	a-rd			1	1			
1801	Kenten, Phillip	a-rd	Licking	- Kentin	1	1		4	
1801	Kimbrough, Samuel	b-rd			1	1	1	1	
1801	Kimbro, John	b-rd			1	1	14	5	

Year	Person	Location & Water Course	ent/sur	(1)	(2)	(3)	(4)	
1801	Kimbrough, Nathaniel "			1				
1801	Keith, Phillip	N-sd	Ceder Creek	- Kenten	1	2		1	
1801	Keith, Jacob	N-sd			1	1		1	
1801	Kays, John	N-sd	Licking		1	1		2	tav
1801	Loughridge, William	a-rd			1	1			
1801	Loughridge, John	a-rd	Sommerset	- Fowler	1	1		8	
1801	Leeper, John	a-rd			1	1	5	8	
1801	Leeper, William	a-rd			1	1		2	
1801	Low, William	b-rd			1	1		2	
1801	Low, George	b-rd	Indian Creek	- Young	1	1		1	
1801	Lilly, Anieger	b-rd	Hinkson	- Reece	1	1	1	2	
1801	Lilly, Pleasant	b-rd			1				
1801	Leavengood, George	b-rd			1	1			
1801	Loan, Isaac	N-sd			1	1		1	
1801	Leonard, Valentine	N-sd	Ceder Creek	- Kenten	1	1		4	
1801	Leonard, Michael	N-sd			1	1		3	
1801	Louderback, Andrew	N-sd			1	1		1	
1801	Livingston, David	N-sd			1	2			
1801	McFerren, William	a-rd			1	1			
1801	McDonald, Mordicay	a-rd			1	1		2	
1801	Morgan, David	a-rd	Brushey Fork	- Fleming	1	1		5	
1801	McMahan, Robert	a-rd	Sommerset	- Halems	1	1	3	2	
1801	Miller, John	a-rd			1	1			
1801	Morgan, John	a-rd	(Montgomery Co.)		1	1		1	
1801	Marsh, Thomas	a-rd	Brushey Fork		1	1	6	3	
1801	Marsh, Dial	a-rd			1	1	7	3	
1801	Mitchel, John	a-rd		- Stockden	1	1		4	
1801	Mathers, William	a-rd	Brushey Fork	- Stockden	1	3		5	
1801	Mathers, Samuel	a-rd			1				
1801	McCune, John	a-rd			1	1		3	
1801	McCune, Robert	a-rd			1	1		3	
1801	Myers, George	a-rd	Cassidy	- Young	1	2		5	
1801	Myers, John	a-rd			1	1		3	
1801	Moore, Samuel	a-rd			1	1	3	1	
1801	Morris, Thomas	a-rd			1	1			
1801	Morgan, Garret	a-rd	Brushey Fork		1	1		1	
1801	McInutty, Joseph	a-rd	Somerset	- Fowler	1	1		3	
1801	Marshall, Archibald	a-rd	Licking	- W. Bell	1	1	2	5	
1801	Marshall, David	a-rd			1	1			
1801	McClannahan, James	a-rd			1	1		1	
1801	McCouns, Sarrenis	a-rd			1				

Year	Person	Location & Water Course		ent/sur	(1)	(2)	(3)	(4)	
1801	McCall, James	a-rd			1	2		1	
1801	Miller, William	a-rd			1	1			
1801	McDonald, George	a-rd			1	1		3	
1801	Mitchel, William	a-rd	Brushey Fork	- Shull	1	1		4	
1801	Mitchel, James	a-rd			1	1		3	
1801	McCormach, James	a-rd	Brushey Fork	- Tiernan	2	2	1	4	
1801	Monhollen, Patrick	a-rd			1			3	
1801	Matlock, Samuel	b-rd			1	1		1	
1801	McGinnis, William	b-rd			1	1			
1801	Menteen, Robert	b-rd			1	1		2	
1801	(McComs/McGuin),Jas.	"			1				
1801	McCracken, John	b-rd	Hinkson	- Young	1	1		1	
1801	McShain, Sarah	b-rd			1	1			
1801	Miller, Abraham	b-rd	Indian Creek	- Young	1	1		4	
1801	McFarland, William	b-rd		- Young	1	2		1	
1801	McIntire, Robert	b-rd	Hinkson	- Cook	1	1	1	4	1s
1801	McDowel, William	b-rd	Fighting	- Gray	1	1		2	
1801	McDowel, Mary	b-rd	Rough Branch	- Rece					
1801	Man, John	b-rd	Brushey Fork	- Ingrams	1	1		1	
1801	McDonal, Alexander	b-rd			1	1		1	
1801	Man, George	b-rd		- Ingrams	2	3		4	
1801	Man, Peter	b-rd			1	1		3	
1801	Man, Jacob	b-rd		- Ingrams	1	1		3	
1801	McGriff, Richard	a-rd			1	2		1	
1801	Mitcheltree, (Jopias)	b-rd			1	1		1	
1801	Murphey, W. George	b-rd			1	1		2	
1801	McClintock, Hugh	b-rd	Hinkson	- H. Thomspn	1	1		1	
1801	McClintock, Joseph	b-rd		- H. Thompsn	1			5	
1801	McCormick, James	b-rd	Wilmers Run	- Young	2	1		1	
1801	McDonald, William	b-rd	Beaver		1	1			
1801	Marshall, Ralph	b-rd	Beaver		1	3		2	
1801	Martain, Zedehiah	b-rd			1	1		5	
1801	Morgan, James	b-rd			1	1			
1801	Mitcheltree, Thomas	b-rd			1	1			
1801	Martain, John	N-sd	Licking	-Johnston	1	3		4	
1801	McCarty, David	N-sd			1	2		4	
1801	McCarty, Thomas	N-sd			1	1			
1801	McCord, William	N-sd			1	1			
1801	McCord, Michael	N-sd			1	1			
1801	McCord, Wm., Sr.	N-sd			1			1	
1801	Mason, Burgess	N-sd			1	3	2	3	

Year	Person	Location & Water Course	ent/sur	(1)	(2)	(3)	(4)
1801	Metcalf, Thomas	N-sd	Ceeder Creek - J. Metcalf	1	2		2
1801	McClintock, Joseph,	N-sd	Ceeder Creek - Kenten	1	1		1
1801	Montcrief, Elizabeth	N-sd	(Campbell Co.)		1		3
1801	Morris, Jacob	N-sd	Ceeder Creek - Kenten	1	1		1
1801	McCracken, John	N-sd		1	1		3
1801	McClurgh, Joseph	N-sd		1	1		3
1801	Morgan, Joseph	N-sd		1	1		
1801	Metcalf, Eli	N-sd	Johnston - Walden	1	1	4	3
1801	McCord, David	N-sd		1	1		2
1801	Morgan, Charles	N-sd		1			1
1801	McKinley, George	N-sd		1	1		
1801	Nucum, Daniel	a-rd		1	1		1
1801	Nesbet, Nathan	a-rd	- Fleming	1	1	1	5
1801	Nesbet, Thomas	a-rd	Brushey Fork - Fleming	1	1		3
1801	Nickel, Robert	a-rd		1	1		
1801	Nesbet, Samuel	a-rd		1			
1801	Nudigate, William	N-sd	Johnston - Thornton	1	2		3
1801	Oden, William	N-sd		1	1	3	1
1801	Oliver, John	N-sd	Ceder Creek - Kenten	2	2		4
1801	Palmer, Robert	a-rd		1	1	1	2
1801	Peyton, Thomas	a-rd		1	1		
1801	Potts, Frederick	a-rd			1		
1801	Paxton, Robert	a-rd		1	1		3
1801	Potts, William	a-rd	Somerset - Fowler	1	1	4	4
1801	Peyton, Samuel	a-rd		1	1		
1801	Pendergrass, Edward	a-rd		1			
1801	Plew, Jeremiah	a-rd	Somerset - Fowler	1	1		2
1801	Polley, John	a-rd	- Coxes	1	2		3
1801	Parks, Joseph	a-rd		1	1	1	2
1801	Pough, Henry	a-rd		1	1		1
1801	Parks, Robert	a-rd		1	1	1	4
1801	Plew, Elias	a-rd	- Fowler	2	2		1
1801	Powel, Thomas	a-rd	Somerset - Abercrumy	2	3		12
1801	Peyton, William	a-rd		1			
1801	Powel, Charles	a-rd		1	1		1
1801	Parks, James for John Lisle	a-rd	Brushey Fork - Myars Somerset	1	1	1	2
1801	Peyton, Stephen	a-rd	- S. Noble	1	1		2
1801	Pumel, William	b-rd		1	1		
1801	Porter, Thomas	b-rd		1	1		1
1801	Porter, John	b-rd		1	1		1

Year	Person	Location & Water Course	ent/sur	(1)	(2)	(3)	(4)
1801	Perren, C. William	N-sd	(Harison Co.)	2	2	1	2
1801	Protchet, William	N-sd	Licking	- Henry	1	1	2	1
1801	Robeson, James	a-rd	Brushey Fork	- Halims	1	1	1	4
1801	Riddel, William	a-rd	Brushey Fork	- Halims	1	1		1
1801	Razor, Henry	a-rd			1	1		
1801	Ray, James	a-rd			1			6
1801	Ray, Frances	a-rd		- Stockden	1	1		3
1801	Reed, William	a-rd	Brushey Fork	- Halims	1	2		2
1801	Robeson, Abraham	a-rd			1	1		
1801	Roberts, Neily	a-rd	Somerset	- Fowler	1	1		2
1801	Roberts, Henly	a-rd	Somerset	- Fowler	1	1		2
1801	Reily, John	a-rd	Somerset	- Fowler	1	1		4
1801	Reviel, Joseph	a-rd	Cassidy	- Cassiday	1	1		1
1801	Robeson, Samuel	a-rd			1			3
1801	Rhoads, Becham	a-rd	Licking	- Cassdy	1	1		2
1801	Rolsten, Samuel	a-rd			1	1		
1801	Reed, Isaac	a-rd			1	1		
1801	Roberts, (W. Jonah)	a-rd			1	1		1
1801	Roberts, Hezekiah	a-rd			1	1		
1801	Robeson, Joseph	a-rd			1	1		
1801	Richey, Robert	b-rd	Willmers Run	- Cook	1	1		1
1801	Ruby, Joseph	b-rd	Indian Creek		1	1		1
1801	Ragsdale, Drury	N-sd			1			
1801	Ray, Samuel	N-sd			1			
1801	Shannon, Samuel	a-rd	Indian Creek		1	1		
1801	Shaw, John	a-rd			1	1		3
1801	Shannon, Thomas	a-rd	Somerset	- Fowler	1	1		2
1801	Sanderson, James	a-rd	Somerset	- Fowler	1	1	1	3
1801	Shankland, John	a-rd	Cassdy	-Gates/Cassidy	1	1	1	2
1801	Stephenson, William	a-rd			1	1		3
1801	Sample, Robert	a-rd			1	1		1
1801	Scott, Thomas	a-rd			1	1		
1801	Sanderson, John	a-rd	Licking		2	2		1
1801	Sanderson, John, Jr.	a-rd			1	1		3
1801	Stephenson, Robert	a-rd			1	1		1
1801	Stephenson, James	a-rd	Somerset	- Fowler	1	1		3
1801	Snap, George	b-rd			1	1		2
1801	Snap, John	b-rd				1		1
1801	Stewart, John	b-rd	HInkson	- Rece	1			2
1801	Stephenson, Thomas	b-rd		- Young	1	1		5
1801	Stephenson, (Marow)	b-rd	Indian Creek	- Stephenson	1	1	6	4

24

Year	Person	Location &	Water Course	ent/sur	(1)	(2)	(3)	(4)	
1801	Stubs, Anny	b-rd		- Crawford			2	6	
1801	Stewart, Joseph	b-rd		- Young	1	1		2	
1801	Scott, Moses	b-rd			1	1		1	
1801	Scott, Mathew	b-rd			1	1		5	
1801	Scott, Gabriel	b-rd			1				
1801	Scott, Thomas	b-rd			1	1		2	
1801	Scott, John	b-rd		- Young	1	1		1	
1801	Summet, George	b-rd			1	1		5	
1801	Summet, Christian	b-rd	Hinkson	- Sumet	1			5	
1801	Snap, Peter	b-rd			1	1		2	
1801	Shillinger, Adam	b-rd	Brushey Fork	- Ingram	1	1		4	
1801	Sadler, John	b-rd	Hinkson	- Cook	1	1		1	
1801	Seldon, Roger	b-rd			1				
1801	Sandiford, Nathan	N-sd	Licking		1	1	7	8	
1801	Scott, Solomon	N-sd	Johnston	- Harison	1	1		3	
1801	Smith, John	N-sd			1	1		2	
1801	Stewart, Mathew	N-sd			1	1			
1801	Standiford, Elijah	N-sd			1	1		1	
1801	Standiford, Aquila	N-sd	Licking	- Martain	1	1			
1801	Smith, William	N-sd			1	1		1	
1801	Sandiford, George	N-sd			1	1	1	7	
1801	Stewart, James	N-sd			1	1			
1801	Sworden, Quinten	N-sd			1	1		2	
1801	Sanders, Hezekiah	N-sd	Johnston	- Johnston	1	1		1	
1801	Stewart, Willaby	N-sd			1	1		2	
1801	Shively, John	N-sd			1	1			
1801	Spaw, Henry	N-sd			1	1		3	
1801	Sheepherd, John	N-sd			1	1		1	
1801	Stockdel, James	N-sd			1	2		2	
1801	Stoop, George	N-sd			1	1		1	
1801	Toppins, Robert	a-rd			1	1			
1801	Thompson, Joseph	a-rd			1	1	2		
1801	Thompson, William	a-rd			1	1		4	
1801	Thompson, Alex.	a-rd			1	1		2	
1801	Thompson, James, Jr.	a-rd	Somerset	- Fowler	2	1		7	
1801	Thomas, Edward	b-rd	Wilmers Run	- A. Moor	1	1		2	
1801	Tully, John	b-rd			1	1		3	
1801	Trousdale, John	b-rd	Indian Creek	- Young	1	1			
1801	Trousdale, William	b-rd			1	1		1	
1801	Thomson, Henry	b-rd	Hinkson	- M. Thompsn	1	2		8	
1801	Tate, Francis	b-rd			1				

Year	Person	Location & Water Course		ent/sur	(1)	(2)	(3)	(4)	
1801	Throckmorton, Thos.	N-sd	Licking		1		8	1	
1801	Throckmorton, Thos., Jr.	"			1				
1801	Taylor, L. John	b-rd			1	1			
1801	Taylor, Thomas	b-rd			1	1			
1801	Taylor, James	N-sd	Ceder Creek		1	1		2	
1801	Taylor, Thomas, Jr.	N-sd			1	1		2	
1801	Taylor, Joseph	N-sd			1	1		1	
1801	Taylor, William	N-sd			1	1		2	
1801	Tate, James	N-sd			1				
1801	Veach, John	a-rd			1	1		1	
1801	Vaughn, Thomas	a-rd			1	1	9	10	
1801	Vanhook, Archiles	b-rd	Indian Creek	- Young	1	1		2	
1801	Vanhook, Abner	b-rd	Indian Creek	- Crawford	1	1		1	
1801	Varner, Koonrod	b-rd			1	1		3	
1801	Venoy, Francis	N-sd	Johnston	-Montgomery	1	2	1	3	
1801	Vaughn, Daniel	N-sd	Johnston		1	1			
1801	Willson, Benjamin	a-rd			1	2		2	
1801	West, Amos	a-rd			1	1	5	3	
1801	West, Isaac	a-rd	Cassidy	- Cassidy	1	1		4	
1801	Williams, John	a-rd	Somerset	- Fowler	1	1		1	
1801	Wesbter, Topias	a-rd			1	1			
1801	Wills, John	a-rd			1	1		1	
1801	Waugh, Samuel	a-rd	Brushey Creek - West		1	1	1	4	
1801	Williams, Hubbard	b-rd			1	1	9	3	
1801	Webb, Anny	a-rd	Hinkson	- Young		1		1	
1801	Waits, John	a-rd	Indian Creek	- Young	1	1		2	
1801	Wisely, William	a-rd			1	1		2	
1801	Waggoner, Christian	a-rd	Indian Creek		1	1		1	
1801	Waggoner, John	a-rd	Beaver		1	1		2	
1801	Wolf, Joseph	N-sd			1	1		4	
1801	Wallace, William	N-sd	Johnston	- Johnston	1	1		5	
1801	Weaver, William	N-sd			1	1		4	
1801	Welch, Abraham	N-sd			1	1	3	4	
1801	West, Thomas	N-sd		- Johnston	1	1		2	
1801	Welch, John	N-sd			1				
1801	Ward, Andrew	N-sd		- Harison	1	1		1	
1801	Wiggons, John	N-sd	Johnston	- Johnston	1	1		5	
1801	Ward, George	N-sd		- Harison	1	1		1	
1801	Watson, James	N-sd	Licking	- Kinten	3	4		2	
1801	Wheeler, William	N-sd			1	1			
1801	Willon, Benjamin	N-sd			1	1		4	

| 1801 | Young, Jacob | b-rd | | 1 | 1 | 5 |

Total number of voters   502

Certified list of taxable property taken by Commissioner
James Parks 3rd October 1801
Clerk Lewis H. Arnold

WHO WERE THE WOMEN

Few women appear in frontier records. It was simply an era when men handled all legal affairs. The women in these tax lists are usually widows. Some have enough money to remain unmarried and appear on the lists with their sons. Others disappear and soon as they can remarry.

Adams, Hannah - probably widow of Thomas or William
Anderson, Sarah - probable widow of James
Beard, Mary   - probable widow of John
Bell, Jane   - wealthy - 9 years
Bell, Jane   - daughter of Jane
Blair, Sarah   - is she a daughter of Alexander?
Bradley, Susanna- no indication
Brooks, Susanna - wife of William & mother of Zachariah?
Buchanan, Pheobe- wife of Jonathan or William
Cochran, Margaret- one entry, but census year - head of household
Craig, Margaret   - mother of John & James?
Crawford, Mary   - wife of John
Dailey, Mary   - sister-in-law to John S.
Duzan, Elizabeth   - possibly a daughter
Evans, Rachel   - John is missed the year she is recorded
Forsyth, Jean   -sister-in-law ?
Glasscock, Cena & Peggy - were the men moving timber?
Harrison, Anne   - beneficary
Hartley, Elizabeth - maybe wife of Thomas
Jenkins, Mary   - wife of Solomon
Johnson, Jean   - too many choices
Kimbrough, Elizabeth - Nathaniel's widow
Kimbrough, Susanna - Sam's or Richard's
McCormick, Elizabeth- appears to be James's widow
McDanald, Mary   - only missiing male is William
McDowell, Mary and Margaret - mother & daughter ?
McShan, Sarah   - is she mother to Daniel McShain
Montcrief, Elizabeth - four years
Morgan, Agnes   - too many choices
Myers, Margaret   - possibly Jacob
Oliver, Ellizabeth - listed as widow
Paugh, Sarah   - probably Henry
Roberts, Abagail - too many choices
Sample, Mary   - George ?
Standeford, Sarah - Nathan or Elijah
Stephenson, Eliza - ?
Stewart, Mary   - ?
Stockwell, Ann   - James   - several others with just one entry

NICHOLAS COUNTY TAX LIST
1809
Handwriting & ink very poor - (questionable)
(actually 2 lists - one entitled "Revised")
(list #2 is almost illegible)   (bracketed names best guess)

Year	Person	Location & Water Course	ent/sur	(1)	(2)	total blacks (3)	(4)	
1809	Allison, John	Johnson	R. Johnson	1			4	
1809	Ashbrook, Thomas	Indian		1			6	
1809	Ashcraft, Jacob	Little Beaver	Monroe	1			1	
1809	Ashcraft, Ephraim	"		1			4	
1809	Asbury, William, Sr.	"	Henry	1		5	6	
1809	Asbury, William, Jr.	"		1			4	1s
1809	Allison, Alex.	"		1			2	
1809	Asberry, Henry	"		1		3	6	
1809	Anderson, John	Ceder Creek	Hawatt	1			6	
1809	Artt, William, Jr.			1			1	
1809	Artt, William, Sr.	Johnson	Bodly	3			5	
	A(revised) - much of this list is illedgible							
1809	Abraham, (Moriseth)			1			1	
1809	Arnett, Samuel	Brushey Fork	Garnett	1		3	5	1s
1809	Anderson, James	Indian Creek	Fowler	1			2	
1809	Anderson, George	Cassiday	"	1				
1809	(Alexander, Jesse)		"	1				
1809	(A------, James)			1				
1809	(Ardery, Robert)			1			4	
1809	Ardery, James	(Thornton)		1			3	
1809	Allen, William	Swearingin						
1809	Archer, Sampson			1				
1809	(Archer, John, Sr.)		West	1			4	
1809	(Archer, John, Jr.)		Fowler	1			3	
1809	(Asbury, William, Sr.)	Little Bever		1		13	30	
1809	(A-------, ----------)							
1809	(A-------, ----------)							
1809	(A-------,----------)							
	B							
1809	Bradly, Robt.			1			3	
1809	Brown, James	Indian Creek		1			3	
1809	Brown, John	"		1			4	
1809	Ball, James	"		1			4	
1809	Baker, John	Steels Run		1		6	4	
1809	(Beall), John	Indian		1			2	

Year	Person	Location & Water Course	ent/sur	(1)	(2)	(3)	(4)
1809	Baker, Martin	(Steels Run)		1		1	6
1809	(Baker), John			1			3
1809	(Branon), Thomas	Ceder Creek	Henry	1			6
1809	(Branon), John	"		1			2
1809	Brady, ------			1			3
1809	Brady, George	"		1			4
1809	Brady, Elisha			1			2
1809	Brown, John	Johnston		1		2	3
1809	Boggess, Thomas	Indian Creek	R. Johnston	1		2	7
1809	Bartlett, William	Licking	Bell	1			12
1809	Bartlett, Ebenzer		Young	1			5
1809	Bartlett, Samuel			1			4
1809	Bartlett, Joseph			1			2
1809	(Biles), John	Bever	Ervin	1			3
1809	Bedinggall, David	Licking	Bell	1		7	13
1809	Baker, James			1		3	2
1809	Buckler, Robt.			1			1
1809	Brown, Alex.			1			3
1809	Brinson, Jonathan	Beaver Creek		1			3
1809	Busby, William		Young	1			2
1809	Busby, Archibald	Johnson		1			1
1809	Bentley, Michael		Bodley	1			3
1809	Bailey, Basel			1			2
1809	Buchanan, Peobe B (revised)	Johnston	Thornton			5	5
1809	Buckner, Samuel	(Sumerset)		1			1
1809	Buntin, Andrew		Fowler	1			2
1809	Brown,(James)	Steals Run		1			6
1809	(Brinton,------)			2			2
1809	(Baker,-------)		"	1			1
1809	(Barnett, Ambrose)		Grisnot				
1809	(Barnett, John)			1			1
1809	(Brooks, Susanna)	Wilmers Run				2	4
1809	(Barlow, John)			1			5
1809	(Barlow, William)			1		1	6
1809	(Baskett, Jesse)					5	5
1809	(Buckner, James)		D.Hall	1			1
1809	(Brinton, ------)			1			3
1809	(B------, James)			1			
1809	(Barnes, John)	Cassady		1			3
1809	(Brown, H----)						3

Year	Person	Location & Water Course	ent/sur	(1)	(2)	(3)	(4)	
1809	(Brown, Ja----)	Somerset		1			1	
1809	(Brown, Ja----)			1				
1809	(Barnett, William)			1			4	
1809	(Barlow, David)			1				
1809	(Bennington, Nehemiah)	Brush Fork	Stockton	1			2	
1809	(B------, ------)	Summerset	Fowler	1	4	7		
1809	(Baker, Jacob	Brush Fork		1			1	
1809	(B-----,-------)		Fleming	1			2	
1809	(B-----,-------		Fowler				1	
1809	(Buntin, James)	Summerset		1			3	
1809	(Baler, John)			1			3	
1809	(Bowen, William)							
1809	(Boteman, Henry)			1			4	
1809	(Bryam, August)	(Flatt Creek)	Fowler	1			1	
1809	((Bradshaw, David)	Brushey Fork		1			3	
1809	(Boles, William)			1				
1809	(Brown, John)						2	
	C							
1809	Caha, John	Licking	Combs	3			2	
1809	Cack, David	Little Bever	Kenton	1			4	
1809	Collings, (Eunincy)	Licking	Kenton	1		1	4	
1809	Collier, (Claiborne)			1		3	3	
1809	Crips, William T.			1			4	
1809	Conaway, John	Steels Run	Conway	1		3	5	
1809	(Cowan, Samuel)	Sider	Kenton	1			2	
1809	Collings, Stephen			1			1	
1809	(Cord, Bethiah)						1	
1809	Cosby, Fowler			1			1	
1809	Carthers, Thomas	Indian Creek	Young	1			10	
1809	Culp, Thomas	Beaver	Thomas	1			2	
1809	Chaney, James			1		3	4	
1809	Collier, Hamlett			1		3	6	
1809	Cord, Richard			1			1	
1809	Carter, Daniel			1				
1809	Coobia, Thomas	Stoney Creek	W. Bell	1		4	1	1s
1809	Clark, Benjamin	Johnson	Johnson	2		11		1s
1809	Cassabaugh, Ester	Indian Creek (added at end)					5	
	C (revised) ink very poor							
1809	(Car---,------)						1	
1809	Clay, William	Brush Fork	Cook	1		3	5	6s
1809	(C------,------)			1				

Year	Person	Location & Water Course	ent/sur	(1)	(2)	(3)	(4)	
1809	(C---well,----)						1	1s
1809	(Cororn, Isaac)	Cassady	Yates	1			4	
1809	Carnahan, Robert	Licking	Young	1			3	
1809	(Canady, Robert)			1			2	
1809	Carter, Jonathan			1			3	
1809	Campbell, James	Flatt Creek	Fowler	1			3	
1809	Caldwell, Thomas	Cassady	Fowler				1	
1809	(C------,------)						1	
1809	(Claney, James)	(Flatt Creek)	Cook	1		2	3	
1809	Claney, William			1				
1809	(Cotral, Thomas)	Steals Run	(Christy)	1				
1809	Crawford, William	Brush Fork	Myers	1			2	
1809	Crawford, Mary						4	
1809	Crawford, (Samuel)			1			5	
1809	(Casady, James)	Summerset	(Fowler)	1			3	
1809	Caldwell, David			1			3	
1809	Caldwell, (-----)			1			6	
1809	(C-------,-------)			1		3	3	
1809	(C-------,-------)			1			3	
1809	(C-------,-------)			1			1	
1809	(C-------), William			1				
1809	(C-------,-------)			1			2	
1809	(Caldwell,------)	Cassady	Thornton	1			5	
1809	(C------,-------)			1				
1809	(C------,-------)			1				
1809	(C------,-------)			1				
1809	(C------,-------)			1			3	
1809	(Carnahan, James)			1			2	
1809	Casady, James	Cassady	Fowler	1			2	
1809	Carnahan, James. (M.)			1			4	
1809	Caldwell, (Walter)	Licking	Dawson	1		3	4	
1809	Clark, John, Jr.			1			1	
1809	Clark, John, Sr.	Summersett	Swearingen	1			7	
1809	Cassady, Daniel	"	Fowler	1			3	
1809	Corbin, Nathan			1			1	
1809	Caldwell, (Robert)	"	"	1			4	
1809	Clark, William			1			3	
1809	Collier, Franklin			1		1	2	

D

Year	Person	Location & Water Course	ent/sur	(1)	(2)	(3)	(4)	
1809	Daisey, John			1			2	
1809	Dagley, Mary	Little Beaver	Kenton			2	3	

Year	Person	Location & Water Course	ent/sur	(1)	(2)	(3)	(4)
1809	Dunkin, Joseph	"	Kenton	1		4	5
1809	Dunkin, James			1			
1809	(Duzan, Elizabeth)	Little Beaver		1		4	6
1809	(Davis, William)			2			6
1809	(Davis, Robert)			1			5
1809	(Duzan, John)			1			1
1809	Douhety, (Jesse)			1		1	1
1809	Dunkin, William	Little Beaver	Henry	1		4	4
1809	Davis, Thomas			1			
1809	Duzan, Jacob	Licking	Moseby	1			5
1809	Duzan, William			1			2
	D (revised) ink very poor						
1809	Doughty, John	Summerset	Fowler	1			1
1809	Doughty, Thomas	Cassady	Bell	1			5
1809	(Doughty), James	Licking	Young	1			2
1809	Dinsmore, Henry	Brush Fork	Haws	1			1
1809	Dingle, William			1			4
1809	Datson, James						
1809	Dial, Mathew			1		3	2
1809	Dinsmore, John	Brush Fork	Morgan	2			6
1809	(D------), John				1		
1809	(D------), Alexander			1		1	2
1809	Dinsmore, James	Steals Run		1			2
1809	Darling, Abraham	Brush Fork		1			3
1809	Dmitt, Henry			2			2
1809	Dmitt, Jacob			1			1
1809	Davidson, Thomas	Summerset	Fowler	1			5
1809	Downey, (John)	Cassady	Fowler	1			3
1809	Davidson, John	Brush Fork	Fowler	1			3
1809	Doughty, William			1			2
1809	Dayton, Garret			1			3
	E						
1809	Eaton, Isaac			1			2
1809	Eastes, Thomas	Indian Creek	Young	1			5
1809	Eaton, Jacob	Johnston		1			4
1809	Ellis, John			1			2
1809	Ellerbeck, Joseph			1		3	2
1809	Eaton, John			1			5
1809	(------------)			1			1
	E (revised) ink very poor						
1809	Enlow, Jesse	Brush Fork	Noble	1		2	3

Year	Person	Location & Water Course	ent/sur	(1)	(2)	(3)	(4)	
1809	(Earlwine), Daniel			1			5	
1809	(Earlwine), Jacob			1			4	
1809	(Earlwine), George	Wilmores Run	Hawes	1			3	
1809	(E--------, ------)	Stoney Fork	Bell	1		2	2	
1809	Ellis, James			1			2	
1809	Ellis, William						1	
1809	(Edwards), William			1				
1809	Evans, John			1			2	
1809	Edwards, Hannah					4	1	
	F							
1809	Fight, Jacob			1			2	
1809	Fryman, Philip, Sr.	Bever	Ervin	1			4	
1809	Fryman, Philip, Jr.			1			2	
1809	Fieles, William			1			1	
1809	Fielder, George	Johnson	Johnson	1		10	8	
1809	Fowler, James			1			4	
1809	Fields, Ebenzer	Licking	Kenton	1			4	
1809	Feeback, Fredrick	Beaver Creek	John Young	1			2	
	F (revised) ink very poor							
1809	(Foster), Thomas						2	
1809	(Foster), Harrison			1			4	
1809	(F------), James			1			3	
1809	(F------), Hugh			1			9	
1809	Fulton, John			1			2	
1809	Fulton, Samuel	Brush Fork	Fleming	1			2	
1809	(Fim), James			1				
1809	Fryman, George			1			3	
1809	(F-----), John	Summerset	Fowler	1			3	
1809	Fitzpatrick, Jos.			1			1	
1809	Fuller, Joseph			1				
1809	Fowler, Luke (listed in "T"s			1			3	
	G							
1809	Gray, David	Johnston	Johnston	1		2	5	
1809	(Gambriel, Thomas)	Sider	Kenton				1	
1809	(Gwaithins, James)			1			5	
1809	(Gwaithins, Thomas)			2				
1809	(Griffith, -------)	Indian	C. Young	1			4	
1809	Glen, Elijah	Richland	Kenton	1		3	4	
1809	Grosvenor, Richard	Beaver	J. Young				2	
1809	Gragg, Joseph			1			3	
	G (revised) ink very poor							

Year	Person	Location & Water Course	ent/sur	(1)	(2)	(3)	(4)	
	G (revised) ink very poor							
1809	Galaspie, James	Cassady	Young	1			3	
1809	Griffith, Martin	Steals Run	Conway	1		3	5	
1809	Gambel, David		Young	1			2	
1809	Galbreath, Benjamin, Sr.	Stoney Creek	Bell				4	
1809	Galbreath, Benjamin, Jr.			1				
1809	Galbreath, William			1			5	
1809	Geghagan, John, Jr.	Wilmores Run	Haws	1			2	1s
1809	Gonce, George			1			2	
1809	Geghagan, John		J. Clater	1			3	
1809	Gray, David	Summerset	Fowler	1			4	
1809	(G----man), William			1			1	
1809	(Glen, Simone)			1		1	1	
1809	(Githen, -------)	Wilmores Run	Haws	1			5	
1809	Gray, Isaac			1			5	
1809	Green, David			1			2	
1809	Green, Zachariah			1			1	
1809	Gorman, Daniel	Cassady	(Horne)	1			1	
1809	Gonce, Nicholas	Steals Run	Kannady	1			2	
1809	Githen, Henry	Wilmores Run	Haws	1			3	
1809	(Gray, William)			1				
	H							
1809	Harney, Hiram			1			4	
1809	Harney, Rolin			1			3	
1809	Howerton, George			2		10	2	
1809	Holler, John	Steels	R. Young	1			2	
1809	(Hardik), John			1			1	
1809	(Harden), Elihu	Licking	Bins	1		3	1	
1809	Harney, Thomas			1			1	
1809	Helpenson, John	Bever	Young					
1809	Honicle, Jacob			1			1	
1809	Howard, Matthew			1			1	
1809	Harney, Mills	Bever		1			1	
1809	Howard, Ephraim			1			6	
1809	Howard, Gidion			1			1	
1809	Hawkins, Samuel	Licking	Owings	1			1	
1809	(Henico, John)			1			2	
1809	(Hisas, Daniel)			1			1	
1809	(Hill, Richard)	Sider Creek	Kenton	1			2	
1809	Holley, Thompson			1			2	
1809	Hildreth, Squire		Owings	1			3	

35

Year	Person	Location & Water Course	ent/sur	(1)	(2)	(3)	(4)	
1809	Holler, John (added at end)							
	H (revised)							
1809	Hill, James	Summerset	Horne	1			4	
1809	Hamilton, Jno.	McBrides	(Stinger)	1			7	
1809	Hudlleston, (-------)	Steals Run	H. Thompson	1			4	1s
1809	Hall, Cornelius	Brush Fork	Haws	1		6	7	
1809	(Hildreth, William)		Haws	1		6	3	1s
1809	(Hudges, Solomon)			1			4	
1809	Hazlett, William	Licking	Cassady	1			1	
1809	(Homes, Jackson)			1			4	
1809	(Haslett, Samuel)	Flat Creek	Kenton	1			4	
1809	Hawkins, Thomas			1			1	
1809	Hawkins, Gregory						1	
1809	Hill, John	Cassady	Kenton	1			6	
1809	Hopkins, Elihue	Brushey Fork		1			2	
1809	Hall, Robert	Summerset	Kenton	1		5	9	
1809	Hall, James	Licking	Kenton	1			1	
1809	Hall, Elihue	Summerset	Kenton	1			6	
1809	Hall, Benjamin	"	Abercromby	1			5	
1809	Huffman, Peter	Hinkston	Abercromby	1			1	
1809	(Ha-----), George			1			1	
1809	Hughes, William			1			5	
1809	Howard, Gideon	Brush Fork	Holmes				2	
1809	Hamilton, Daniel			1			1	
1809	Hall, William	Summerset	Fowler	1			2	
1809	Hartley, Mordica			1			1	
1809	Hinton, Ezekiel		Fowler	1			3	
1809	Hall, Samuel			1			3	
1809	How, Samuel	Summerset	Fowler	1			4	
1809	Howard, Jacob		Fowler	1			4	
1809	Howard. Henry		Fowler	1			4	
1809	Hall, Moses	Brush Fork	Fleming	1			5	
	I							
1809	(Inglis, Peter)	Indian Creek		1			1	
1809	Irvin, Samuel	Beaver Creek	Young	1			2	
	I (revised)							
1809	Ishmael, James			1			1	
1809	Irvin, Andrew	Brush Fork		1			3	
1809	Irvin, Caleb			1			1	
1809	Irvin, Joshua			1			1	

Year	Person	Location & Water Course	ent/sur	(1)	(2)	(3)	(4)
	J						
1809	Johnston, James	Indian Creek		1			4
1809	Jones, Moses	Steels Run		1		8	5
1809	Johnston, Major	"		2			9
1809	Jenkins, William	Licking		1			6
1809	Jenkins, Thomas	Raven Creek		1			1
	J (revised)						
1809	Jolly, David	Flatt Creek	Fowler	1			5
1809	Jones, John	Cassady	Bell	1			2
1809	Javis, George			1			
1809	Jones, Jacob	Brush Fork		1			1
1809	Johnson, Johnathan	Fox Creek	Price	1			1
1809	Jones, Drury			1		1	1
1809	Jones, Jacob			1			1
1809	Johnson, John	Brush Fork		1			3
1809	Jones, John			1			3
1809	Johnson, John, Sr.						3
1809	Johnson, James			1			1
1809	Johnson, William	Bruch Fork		1			3
1809	Jennings, Sollomon			1			4
1809	Jones, (Samuel)			1			1
	K						
1809	Keath, (Philip)	Seder Creek	Kenton	1			9
1809	(Kimbrough, -----)			1			2
1809	Kimbrough, Robt.	Steels Run	Young	1			3
1809	Kimbrough, John	"	Young	1		3	4
1809	Keath, Jacob	Seder Creek	Kenton	1			1
1809	Keath, Adam	Little Beaver	Kenton	1			4
1809	(Ketherwood), Charles	Seder	Kenton	1			6
1809	(Ketherwood), James		(Metcalf)	1			6
1809	Krusor, Michael	"		1			2
1809	Kimbrough, Richard	Steels Run	R. Young				
	K (revised)						
1809	Kincart, James	Brush Fork	Shull	1			2
1809	Kennady, (------)		Bell				3
1809	Kennady, (------)	Licking	Bell	1			3
1809	Kilgor, William	Cassady		1			2
1809	(K------), John				1		4
1809	Kasey, James		Bell	1			2
1809	Kite, John			1			1
1809	Kincart, John	Brush Fork	Haws	1			2

Year	Person	Location & Water Course	ent/sur	(1)	(2)	(3)	(4)	
1809	Kimbrough, Elizabeth	Steals Run	Rice				2	
1809	Kincart, Samuel	Brush Fork	Fleming	1			4	
1809	Kernes, Adam	Summerset	Cox	1			1	
	L							
1809	Lauderback, Andrew	Steels Run	Kenton	1			4	
1809	Livingood, George	Bever	(MCuaco)	1			3	
1809	Lowe, George	Indian Creek	Young	1			4	
1809	Liuzy, David			1			1	
1809	Lilly, Plesant			1		1	6	
1809	Logan, David	Johnson	Walden	1			3	
	L (revised)							
1809	Low, Isaac	Flat Creek	Fowler	1			2	
1809	Long, (Samuel)			1			4	
1809	Lockridge, John	Summerset		2			5	1s
1809	Lockridge, James			1			5	
1809	Lockridge, William			1				
1809	Leeper, John		Fowler	1		6	11	
1809	Leeper, William			1			4	
1809	Lilly, (Amerigo)	Brush Fork		1		1	4	
	M							
1809	Martin, James			1			1	
1809	Morgan, Charles						4	
1809	Maffett, William			1		1	5	
1809	Maffett, Matthew			1			2	
1809	Maffett, Thomas	Steels Run	Young	1		1	4	
1809	Marshal, (James)	Bever	(McCahood)	1			2	
1809	Marshall, Archibald			1			4	
1809	McIntire, Joseph	Sider Creek	Kenton	1		1	8	
1809	(McCune, James)			1				
1809	McConahan, Achilles			1			1	
1809	(Ma------), Thomas	Sider Creek		2		6	6	
1809	Masen, Burges	"		1		8	5	
1809	Masen, Benjamin	"		1			1	
1809	Martin, Nehemiah	Johnson	Johnson	1			4	
1809	Martin, John	"		1			8	
1809	Martin, Samuel			1			4	
1809	McDonnel, Alx.			1				
1809	McDonnel, William			1			1	
1809	McCord, William	Johnston	Bodly	1			3	
1809	McCord, David	Johnston	Bodly	1			2	
1809	McCord, Michael			1				

Year	Person	Location & Water Course	ent/sur	(1)	(2)	(3)	(4)	
1809	McCord, John			1			2	
1809	McCarty, David			1			5	
1809	McCarty, Thomas			1			2	
1809	Miller, Abraham, Sr.	Indian	Young	1			6	
1809	Miller, Abraham, Jr.			1			1	
1809	McFarland, William	"	Crawford	1			3	
1809	McClurg, Joseph	Johnson		1			4	
1809	Metcalf, Eli	"	Walden	2		1	7	
1809	McCabe, Josiah			1		3	2	
1809	Mattox, Elijah	Licking	Moseby	1			4	
	M (revised)							
1809	McNulty, Joseph	Summerset	Fowler	1			7	
1809	(M---sar), John			1			1	
1809	McCall, John			1			1	
1809	Maxwell, William	Brush Fork	Sturgis	1			4	
1809	McClingan, Joseph	Hinkston	Thompson	2			9	
1809	McMahan, Robert	Brush Fork	Henry	1		2	4	
1809	Monicle, Peter			1			2	
1809	Marshall, Hugh			1			2	
1809	Morgan, Garrett	Licking	Young	1			6	
1809	Myers, David		Bell	1			2	
1809	McDanold, John			1			2	
1809	McQuion, Lawrence			1			1	
1809	Myers, George			1			1	
1809	Myers, John			1			3	
1809	Marshal, John			1			2	
1809	Myers, Margaret	Licking	Bell				3	
1809	McIntire, Joseph			1			2	
1809	McCall, James			1			3	
1809	McDanald, Alex	Licking	Bell	1			1	
1809	McCan, William			1			2	
1809	Mann, Jacob	Brush Fork	Ingram	1			5	
1809	Mann, John			1			4	
1809	Mann, Peter				1		4	1s
1809	(M------, A----)	Flate	Clark			1		
1809	McClintock, Hugh	Hinkston	Thompson	2			5	
1809	Mathers, William, Sr.	Brush Fork	Stockton	1			4	
1809	McCune, Robert			1			2	
1809	Mathers, William, Jr.			1			4	
1809	McCune, Robert, Sr.	McBrides Run	Swearingen	1			3	
1809	Marsh, Thomas	Brush Fork	Proctor	1		8	7	

Year	Person	Location & Water Course	ent/sur	(1)	(2)	(3)	(4)	
1809	(M--------)			1			1	
1809	McDowel, William		Noble	1			9	1s
1809	(M-------, B. Wilson)	Rough Creek	Rice	-				
1809	McGinnis, William	Brush Fork	A. Moor	1			2	
1809	(Mc--------), William			1			3	
1809	(M-------)			1				
1809	(McCormack), Elizabeth		Young				2	
1809	(M-------)			1		3	4	
1809	McCune, John	McBrides Run	Swearingen	1			3	
1809	Mathers, Gaven			1			4	
1809	(M------), Samuel						1	
1809	(M------), Robert			1			2	
1809	(McClinagin, Wm.			1			1	
1809	(McC-------------)						1	
1809	Marshall, (------)			1		2	13	
1809	(M-------), William			1			2	
1809	(Mear), Samuel			1			3	
1809	McMihil, Thomas			1			1	
1809	(McC-----), William	Cassady	Fowler	1			2	
1809	(McDanold, Joseph)		Cassady	1			6	
1809	Murphy, George	Brush Fork	Cook					
1809	Monicle, Christopher			1			5	
1809	McLaughlin, John			1			3	
1809	(Mansire), Samuel			1			5	
1809	(Mannan), Kenneth			1			2	
1809	Moler, Isaac	Summerset	Dupree	1			3	
1809	Miller, James			1			2	
1809	Murphy, Zephimal	Summerset	Dupree	1			7	
1809	McClain, Charles		Fowler	1			2	
1809	(Merit), Thomas	"	Fowler	-				
1809	McNulty, James			1			1	
1809	McNulty, John			1			1	
1809	Marshall, David	Summerset	Fowler	1			3	
1809	McCoy, Daniel		Fowler	1			2	
1809	Mitcheltree, Josia			2			4	
1809	McDanald, George	Licking	Bell	1			1	
1809	McClingan, James	(Three Mile)	Bell	1			6	
1809	Mann, Henry			1			1	
	N							
1809	Nudigate, William	Johnston		1			6	
1809	Nudigate, John			1			2	

Year	Person	Location & Water Course	ent/sur	(1)	(2)	(3)	(4)	
	N (revised)							
1809	Nesbitt, Thomas	Brush Fork	Fleming	1			6	
1809	Nesbitt, Nathan		Fleming	1			9	
1809	Nickle, Robert			1			1	
1809	(N----, Joseph)			1			3	
	O							
1809	Overfield, Moses	Johnston	Kenton	1			3	
1809	Overbee, Henry	"		1		2	5	
1809	Oliver, John	"		1			3	
	O (revised) none							
	P							
1809	Pritchet, William	Little Bever	Kenton	1		5	2	
1809	Packer, John			1			1	
1809	Pursly, Thomas	Seder Creek		1			2	
1809	Powel, Milley						3	
1809	Philips, Leonard			1				
1809	Prator, Jeremiah			1			3	1s
1809	Parks, James			1			1	
1809	Prator, Zephariah			1				
1809	Prator, Jeremiah, Sr.			1		3	2	
1809	Prater, Ashford			1				
	P (revised)							
1809	Porter, William			1			2	
1809	Powel, Isaac			1			2	
1809	Powel, Charles	Flatt, Creek	Fowler	1			4	
1809	Pendergrass, Edward			1			2	
1809	(Pervet), Thomas	Summerset	Abercromby	1			8	
1809	Powel, Jeremiah			1		1	2	
1809	Purnal, William	Brush Fork	Cook	1		1	4	
1809	Payton, Stephen		Noble	1			4	
1809	(Pervet, Zenue)		Fowler	1			4	
1809	Purnal, Henry			1				
1809	Payton, Samuel			1			2	
1809	Payton, (Stephen)			1			2	
1809	Patton, Jesse			1				
1809	Paton, Robert			1			1	
1809	Payton, Thomas			1			3	
1809	Paxton, Robert	Brush Fork	Fowler	1			6	
1809	Pawley, John			1			3	
1809	Pawley, Isaac			1			1	
1809	(Pawley), William			1			3	

Year	Person	Location & Water Course	ent/sur	(1)	(2)	(3)	(4)	
1809	Prather, Benjamin			1			1	
1809	Powel, Thomas			1			6	
1809	Potts, William	Summerset	Fowler	1	2	6		
1809	Pleugh, Jeremiah	Summerset	Fowler	1			3	
1809	Pleugh, Daniel			1			2	
1809	Patton, Robert, Sr.			1		2	2	
1809	Poe, William	Summerset	Fowler	1			2	
1809	Padget, Daniel						1	
1809	Powel, John			1			4	
1809	Pleugh, Elias	Summerset	Fowler	1			3	
1809	Pawley, John	Summerset	Cox	1			3	
1809	(P------), John			1			4	
	Q (revised)							
1809	Qualer, John			1			2	
	R							
1809	(Rafter, Asain)			1			2	
1809	Rankin, Moses	Licking	R.Robertson	1			3	
1809	(Ritche, Asaph)	Little Bever	D. Young	1			2	
1809	(Ritche), Isaac	"	Young	1				
1809	Ross, Allexander			1			4	
	R (revised)							
1809	Robertson, John	Brush Fork	Helms	1			2	
1809	Robertson, James		Helms	1		2	3	
1809	Rhodes, Silas	Licking	Fowler	1			1	
1809	Rhodes, Benjamin		Gates	1			3	
1809	Rannals, Richard	Flat Creek	Fowler	1			3	
1809	Robertson, Samuel		Horne				3	
1809	Ritchy, William		Horne	1			4	
1809	Roberts, Henly	Summerset	Fowler	1			4	
1809	Reveal, Thomas			1			2	
1809	Reveal, Michael	Brush Fork	Haws	1			2	
1809	Ritchy, Robert		Canady	1			3	
1809	Ray, James			1			3	
1809	Ray, Francis		Stockton	2			11	
1809	Roberts, William			1				
1809	(R------ing), William			1			2	
1809	Roberts, Hezekiah	Summerset	Cox	1			1	
1809	(Ruley), John	Cassady	Fowler	1			8	
1809	Redding, William			1			1	
1809	Ramsey, Archibald			1				
1809	Roberts, Thomas			1			3	

Year	Person	Location & Water Course	ent/sur	(1)	(2)	(3)	(4)	
1809	Reveal, Joseph	Brush Fork	(Myers) 1			4		
1809	(R-----), Solomon			1			1	
1809	(Ritchy), Noah			1			1	
	S							
1809	(Sater). John			1			5	
1809	(Sloop), Joseph			1			2	
1809	(Shipherd), John			1				
1809	Smith, William			1			4	
1809	Swart, James			1			1	
1809	Spaw, Jacob			1			1	
1809	Standiford, George			1			3	
1809	Stogdale, William			1			2	
1809	Stogdale, James		Bodly			2		
1809	Smith, James	Bever	Ervin	1			1	
1809	Standiford, Quilly	Brush Fork	Haws	1			6	
1809	Smith, Ezekiah	Indian Creek	Johnston	1			5	
1809	Swain, Nathan	Johnston	(Moseby)	1			3	
1809	(S-----), William			1			1	
1809	Stewart, Joseph	Indian Creek	Johnston	1			4	
1809	Spaw, Henry			1			1	
1809	Stewart, Willby	Seder Creek	(Madely)	1			3	
1809	Stephenson, Thomas	Steels Run	Young	2			9	
1809	Scott, Matthew	Indian Creek		1		1	6	
1809	Scott, Thomas			1			4	
1809	Standeford, John		Owings	1			4	
	S (revised)							
1809	Sanderson, John	Licking	Young	1			8	
1809	(Summerset), Christian	Hinkston		1			5	
1809	(Summerset), George			1			4	
1809	Stockwell, John	Brush Fork	Young	2			2	1s
1809	Sadler, John		Haws	1			2	
1809	Stoops, Philip	Cassady	Gates	1			5	
1809	Shankland, John		Gates	1			6	
1809	Shankland, James			1			1	
1809	Stephenson, Robert		Fowler	1			3	
1809	Summerville, Richard	Flat Creek	Fowler	1			3	
1809	Smith, (Abrah)			1			1	
1809	Sutton, Elizabeth			1			2	
1809	(Shaps), John	Brush Fork		1		3	2	
1809	Shannon, John			1			4	
1809	Shillinger Adam		Ingram	1			5	

Year	Person	Location & Water Course	ent/sur	(1)	(2)	(3)	(4)	
1809	Snap, John			1			1	
1809	(Star), Hollidy			1		2	2	
1809	Snap, Peter	Hinkston	Cook	1			6	
1809	Snap, Daniel						1	
1809	Snap, Samuel			1			1	
1809	Smith, (Mitchel)			1			2	
1809	(S----), Mary	Steals Run	Rice			2		
1809	Stephenson, James	Summerset	Fowler	1			2	
1809	Stephenson, (Robert, Jr.)						2	
1809	Scott, Thomas	Cassady	Fowler	1			2	
1809	(Stephenson), William	Summerset	Fowler				5	
1809	Scott, Andrew	Cassady	Cassady	1			2	
1809	Stephenson, Joseph	Flat Creek	Fowler	1			1	
1809	Snap, George	Brush Fork	Cook	1			5	
1809	Sharp, (------)			1			3	
1809	(S-----), (Jesse)			1			1	
1809	(Smith, John)	Summerset	Fowler	1			2	
1809	(S-----), William		Cox	1			1	
1809	(S-----), James		Fowler	1			3	
1809	Scott, John	Summerset	Fowler	1			1	
1809	Scott, Thomas, Sr.			1			1	
1809	Shannon, Samuel			1				
1809	Shannon, Margaret		Fowler				2	
1809	Smith, David		Fowler	1			3	
1809	(S------), Robert		Fowler	1			3	
1809	Smith, Hugh			1			2	
	T							
1809	Taylor, George	Seder Creek	Kenton	1			2	
1809	(T-----), Thomas			1		2		
1809	Thogmorton, Thomas, Sr.	Licking	Thogmorton	2		15	11	1s
1809	Thogmorton, John		Henry	1		8		
1809	Taylor, Richard	Indian Creek		1			4	
1809	Taylor, John	Little Bever	Henry	1			3	
1809	Taylor, Tapley			1			1	
1809	Taylor, Nathaniel			1			3	
1809	(Towhair, Nathan)	Indian Creek	Johnston	1			3	
1809	Throckmorton, Thomas Jr.	Licking	Taylor	1		6	7	
	T (revised)							
1809	Taylor, George			1			2	
1809	Tayor, John			1			1	
1809	Thomas, Edward	Wilmers Run	Moore	1			3	

Year	Person	Location & Water Course	ent/sur	(1)	(2)	(3)	(4)	
1809	(Fowler, Luke)	Brush Fork	Garnett	1		3	4	
1809	Thompson, Henry	Hinkston	Thompson	2		1	4	
1809	Thompson, Daniel		Thompson	1			3	
1809	Thompson, William	Summerset	Fowler	2			9	
1809	Thompson, H. James		Fowler	1			7	
1809	Thompson, Alexander		Fowler	1			5	
1809	Taylor, Joshua			1		2	4	
1809	Thompson, Sarah					3	3	
	U							
1809	Ungles, John	Indian Creek	Metcalf	1			1	
	V							
1809	Vanhook, (--tt--)	Indian Creek	Johnston	1			4	
1809	Vanhook, (--echtt)	Indian Creek	Young	1			5	
1809	(Vernde), Hugh			1			2	
1809	Venoy, Francis	Johnson	Bodly	1		1	6	
	V (revised)							
1809	Vaughan, Thomas	Licking	Haycottle	1		10	13	
1809	(Vansdike), Hezekiah			1			7	
	W							
1809	Wills, John	Johnston	Johnston	1			5	
1809	Wiggins, William	"		1			1	
1809	Wiggins, John	"		1			6	
1809	West, Thomas	"		1			7	
1809	Whitly, William			1			1	
1809	Waggoner, John	Bever	McConico	1			5	
1809	Whitley, David			1			1	
1809	Watson, James, Sr.	Little Bever	Henry	1			5	
1809	Watson, James, Jr.	"		1			5	
1809	Wiseman, Hitch			1		2	3	
1809	Wallace, William	Johnston	Johnston	1			4	1s
1809	Williamson, Jas.			1				
1809	(Wi----), James			1			3	
1809	Waugh, Jacob	Johnston	Bodly	1			4	
1809	Woolers, William			1			1	
1809	(Wests), John	Indian Creek	Young	1			4	
1809	Webb, Charles	"	Young	1			2	
1809	Williams, William			1			6	
1809	Whitaker, James	Licking	Moseby	1			3	
	W (revised							
1809	(Webster), (Daniel)			1		1	2	
1809	Worain, Isaac			1			2	

45

Year	Person	Location & Water Course	ent/sur	(1)	(2)	(3)	(4)	
1809	Wills, John	Cassady	Bell	1			3	
1809	West, Isaac		Yates	1			6	
1809	West, Philip			1			1	
1809	Wilson, Charles	Summerset	Abercromby	1		1	6	1s
1809	Waggoner, Christian			1			2	
1809	(West, John)			1			3	
1809	West, Elijah			1			2	
1809	Waugh, James	Brush Fork	Fowler	1		1	3	
1809	Wiley, Samuel			1			5	
1809	West, Amos		Fowler	1		4	8	
1809	Wilson, Isaac			1			4	
1809	Wiley, Johnson			1			5	
1809	Wiley, Hugh	Flatt Creek	Fowler	1			5	
1809	Wiley, William			1			4	
1809	Wiley, John, Jr.			1			4	
1809	Whitecotton, Moses			1			2	
1809	Williams, John	Sumerset	Fowler	1			2	
1809	Wilson, Benjamin	Brush Fork	Young	1			2	

Y

Year	Person	Location & Water Course	ent/sur	(1)	(2)	(3)	(4)	
1809	Young, Alixander			1			2	

Y (revised)

Year	Person	Location & Water Course	ent/sur	(1)	(2)	(3)	(4)	
1809	Yates, Andrew	Summerset	Dupree	2		1	4	
1809	Young, Jacob	Brush Fork	Willing		1		3	

END 1809

NICHOLAS COUNTY
1811 TAX LIST
Hand writing is excellent

Year	Person	Location & Water Course	ent/sur	(1)	(2)	(3)	(4)	
1811	Anderson, Daniel	Summersett	Fowler	1			4	
1811	Anderson, George	"	Cox/Yeager	1			3	
1811	Archer, James	"		1			1	
1811	Alexander, Thomas	Locust					1	
1811	Allen, John	Summersett	John Fowler	1			9	
1811	Anderson, Sally	"	"				3	
1811	Alexander, Jesse	Cassady	E. Gaithers	1			2	
1811	Arnold, Lewis	Licking	W. Bell	1		5	12	
1811	Arnett, Samuel	Brushey Fork	Garnett	1		8	3	
1811	Allison, John	Johnson	Simon Kenton	1			5	
1811	Ashcraft, Ephraim	Beaver	Monro	1			4	
1811	Ashcraft, Jacob	"	"	1			6	
1811	Anderson, John	Ceder Creek	Metcalf	1			5	
1811	Armstrong, Irvin			1			2	
1811	Asberry, Henry	Brinsons Run	Henry	1		7	6	
1811	Asberry, William, Sr.	Little Beaver	Monro	1		5	11	
1811	Asberry, William, Jr.			1				
1811	Allison, Alexander	Ceder Creek	Henry	1			5	
1811	Ardery, Robert			1			3	
1811	Archer, Sampson			1			3	
1811	Allen, William	McBrides Run	Swearingen	1			2	
1811	Ardery, James	Brushey Fork	Stockton	1			6	
1811	Archer, John, Sr.	"	Fowler	1			2	
1811	Archer, John, Jr.	"		1			3	
1811	Art, Thomas	Johnson	Marshall	1			2	
1811	Art, William, Sr.			1			1	
1811	Art, James		Marshall	1			2	
1811	Art, William, Jr.	Johnson		1			2	
1811	Anderson, Edward	"	Moseby	1			5	
1811	Ashly, James P.			1				
	B							
1811	Blair, Alexander	Summerset	Fowler	1			16	
1811	Bunton, Andrew	Cassady	"	1			3	
1811	Bunton, James	Summerset	"	1			7	
1811	Bradshaw, William	"		1			1	
1811	Blout, Reding			1			1	

47

Year	Person	Location & Water Course	ent/sur	(1)	(2)	(3)	(4)	
1811	Bunton, William	Summerset	Fowler	1			6	
1811	Byers, David	Brushey Fork	"	1			6	
1811	Baker, Jacob	"	Thos. Jones	1			3	
1811	Berry, Robert	Summerset	Fowler	1		5	10	
1811	Burris, John	Cassady	Gaither	1			3	
1811	Burris, John	"		1			4	
1811	Boles, William			1			1	
1811	Bowen, William			1			1	
1811	Burnet, William			1			1	
1811	Byram, Augustin	Summerset	Fowler	1		1	6	
1811	Brown, William			1			2	
1811	Burris, James	Taylors Creek	Abercromby	1			1	
1811	Buckner, Samuel	Summerset	Homes	1		5	6	
1811	Brown, James	"	Abercromby	1			4	
1811	Brenton, Robert			1			3	
1811	Brenton, James	"		1			3	
1811	Boyd, John	Summerset	Abercromby	1			7	
1811	Byram, Valentine			1		1	3	
1811	Bedinger, George M.	Licking	Powell/Kenton	1		14	22	
1811	Blackburn, Julius H.			1			2	
1811	Burns, Mathew			1			1	
1811	Boatman, Henry			1			5	
1811	Bell, Jane	Brushey Fork	Fleming				1	
1811	Bradshaw, David	"	Helms	1			4	
1811	Brown, Parker	"		1		1	2	
1811	(Benterd), Josiah	"	Berry	1			6	
1811	Baily, Bendict			1				
1811	Bellis, William			1			1	
1811	Bennington, Nehemiah	Brushey Fork	Stockton	1			2	
1811	Byers, John			1			4	
1811	Busby, Mathew	Beaver	Goodlow	1			4	
1811	Barnet, John			1				
1811	Barnet, Ambrose	Brushey Fork	Garnet	1			4	
1811	Brown, John						3	
1811	Busby, William			1			3	
1811	Barlow, John	Brushey Fork	J. Cook	1			6	
1811	Busby, Archibald			1			1	
1811	Bishop, Terril			1			3	
1811	Brooks, Zachariah	"	J. Claytor	1		3	4	
1811	Brown, Alexander	Indian Creek	R. Johnson	1			4	
1811	Baker, John			1		3	3	

Year	Person	Location & Water Course	ent/sur	(1)	(2)	(3)	(4)
1811	Baker, James			1			1
1811	Barlow, John			1			2
1811	Barlow, Jesse	Indian Creek		1			3
1811	Beater, John		Crawford	1			3
1811	Brown, Jursey		"	1			4
1811	Brown, John			1			4
1811	Bell, Jane		"				5
1811	Boyle, John	Beaver	Goodlow	1		3	
1811	Baskett, Jesse	Hinkston	D. Rece	1		6	7
1811	Baker, Martin		Barksdale	1		8	8
1811	Baker, William	Hinkston	D. Rece	1		6	4
1811	Barlow, William		J. Cook	1		1	7
1811	Ballenger, William			1		1	4
1811	Buckner, Harry	"	Haws	1		5	4
1811	Burdin, Charles	"	D. Rece	1			
1811	Burris, John	Licking	Monro	1			6
1811	Brinson, Thomas, Jr.			1			2
1811	Bradly, David	Ceder Creek	Henry	1			3
1811	Brookin, Robert		Metcalf	1		15	2
1811	Bradly, Robert		Thornton	1			3
1811	Bayley, Basel	Beaver Creek		1			4
1811	Brinson, Thomas, Sr.	Ceder Creek	Monro	1			5
1811	Brinson, Jonathan		Henry	1			3
1811	Duckler, Robert			1			1
1811	Bradly, George			1			
1811	Buckler, Stephen			1			
1811	Bently, James			1			3
1811	Bartlett, Samuel	Licking	W. Bell	1			2
1811	Bartlett, Ebezener	"	W. Bell	1			4
1811	Bently, Michael	Buchanan	Darby/Maree	1			6
1811	Boggess, Thomas	Indian Creek		1		2	4
1811	Bartlett, Joseph			1			2
1811	Bartlett, William	Licking	W. Bell	2			12
1811	Buchanan, Phibe	Johnson	Buckner			5	7
1811	Ballingal, David	Licking	W. Bell	1		1	8
1811	Brown, John	Johnson	Thornton	1		2	4
1811	Brown, Daniel, Sr.			1			2
	C						
1811	Courtney, Elsey			1			2
1811	Cosby, Overton			1			2
1811	Carter, Daniel			1			2

Year	Person	Location & Water Course	ent/sur	(1)	(2)	(3)	(4)	
1811	Collins, Stephen	Johnson	Darby/Maree	1				
1811	Clarke, Benjamin	Johnson	Marshall	2		23	17	1s
1811	Cameron, Samuel	Ceder Creek	Henry	1			5	
1811	Catherwood, Samuel		Metcalf	1			7	
1811	Clarke, David	Little Beaver	Henry	1				
1811	Catherwood, Charles	Ceder Creek	Henry	1			5	
1811	Collier, Clarborne			1		2	6	
1811	Carrothers, Gabriel			1			3	
1811	Conway, John	Hinkston	Conway	1		3	7	
1811	Campbell, John			1			4	
1811	Carrothers, Thomas	Indian Creek	Young	1		1	5	
1811	Clay, Thomas			1				
1811	Cotrill, Thomas		Rece	1			4	
1811	Chainey, William	Hinkston	Goodlow	1		3	2	
1811	Crowehir, William			1		2	3	
1811	Clay, William, Sr.	"	Cook	1		5	7	
1811	Clay, William, Jr.			1			1	
1811	Collier, Hamlett			1		4	6	1s
1811	Clarke, Benjamin			1			1	
1811	Collier, John	Hinkston	Barsdale	1		16	12	
1811	Collier, Coleman			1			2	
1811	Culp, Thomas			1			2	
1811	Collier, Franklin	Brushey Fork	Garnet	1		4	3	
1811	Caughley, John	Licking	Kenton	1			4	
1811	Caughley, David			1			3	
1811	Collins, Edmond	Licking	Kenton	1		1	4	
1811	Coney, Samuel			1			4	
1811	Crawford, Samuel			1			2	
1811	Crawford, Mary	Brushey Fork	Myers				1	
1811	Corbin, Abraham		Haws	1		3	6	
1811	Clarke, William			1			2	
1811	Clarke, John	Summerset	Swearingen	2			12	
1811	Clarke, Jonathan			1			3	
1811	Casey, John	Cassady	Fowler	1			4	
1811	Casey, James	Flat Creek	Fowler	1			4	
1811	Cowan, Hugh	Summersett	Abercromby	1			3	
1811	Campbell, Jonas	Licking	Fowler	2			5	
1811	Carnes, Adam	Summersett	Cox/Fleming	1			7	
1811	Cooper, John			2			6	
1811	Caldwell, Thomas	Cassady	Fowler	1			5	
1811	Cook, Peter			1			2	

Year	Person	Location & Water Course	ent/sur	(1)	(2)	(3)	(4)	
1811	Cowan, Isaac	Cassady	Gather	1			5	
1811	Campbell, Robert			1			4	
1811	Carnahan, James, Sr.			1			4	
1811	Carnahan, James, Jr.			1			4	
1811	Carnahan, Robert	Licking	Young	1			2	
1811	Campbell, James	Cassady		1			3	
1811	Crawford, Alexander			1			1	
1811	Cassady, James			1			4	
1811	Caldwell, David, Sr.	Summerset	Fowler	1			4	
1811	Caldwell, Robert, Jr.			1			2	
1811	Caldwell, William, Jr.		"	2			10	
1811	Cassady, Daniel		"	1			2	
1811	Caldwell, Robert, Sr.	Summerset	"	1			5	
1811	Caldwell, David, Jr.			1			2	
1811	Caldwell, William, Sr.	Summerset		1			2	
1811	Caldwell, Alexander			2			10	
1811	Caldwell, Robert	Cassady	"	1			5	
1811	Campbell, Daniel		"	1			1	
1811	Caughey, John			1			1	
	D							
1811	Duckel, John			1			1	
1811	Davidson, John	Summersett	Fowler	1		1	4	
1811	Davidson, Thomas	"	"	1			5	
1811	Dial, Isaac	"		1			2	
1811	Dial, Abner	"	"	1			2	1s
1811	Dial, Mathew	"		1		3	3	
1811	Darling, Abraham	Brushey Fork	Keever	1			5	
1811	Dinsmore, Henry Sr.			1			2	
1811	Dinsmore, John		Berry	1			7	
1811	Dinsmore, Henry, Jr.	"	Berry	1			3	
1811	Doughty, John			1			2	
1811	Dailey, Leonard	"	Keever	1			4	
1811	Dougherty, John	Licking	Fowler	1			3	
1811	Daten, Garrol			1				
1811	Dougherty, Jesse			1		1	2	
1811	Demit, Henry, Jr			1				
1811	Demit, Henry			1			1	
1811	Demit, Jacob			1			3	
1811	Doughty, William			1			3	
1811	Dotson, James			1			4	
1811	Drummonds, James	Hinkston	Barksdale	1			4	

Year	Person	Location & Water Course	ent/sur	(1)	(2)	(3)	(4)
1811	Davis, Thomas	Hinkston	Young	1			1
1811	Dupree, Thomas			1		1	2
1811	Dingle, William		Goodlow	1			1
1811	Duncan, William	Little Beaver	Henry	1		4	8
1811	Dailey, John	"	"	1		2	7
1811	Duncan, Archibald	"	"	1		4	10
1811	Davis, William	"	"	2		2	5
1811	Davis, Robert		"	1			6
1811	Duncan, James	"		1			2
1811	Duncan, Joseph	"	"	1		7	6
1811	Duzan, William			1			3
1811	Duzan, Jacob	Buchanan	Moseby	1			4
1811	Davidson, Hugh			1		1	4
1811	Downey, Archibald	Cassady	Fowler	1			3
1811	Dowough, James	Licking	Young	1			2
1811	Dolly, Thomas	"		1			3
	E						
1811	Ellis, John			1			
1811	Eaton, Jacob	Five Lick		1			3
1811	Earlewine, Daniel			1			6
1811	Endicott, Jacob	Hinkston	Young	1			2
1811	Earlewine, Jacob			1			1
1811	Eastes, Thomas	Indian Creek	Young	1		1	6
1811	Earlick, Joseph			1			
1811	Earlewine, George	Brushey Fork	Cook	1			5
1811	Evans, Rachel						1
1811	Ellerback, Joseph			1		3	4
1811	Enlow, Jesse	Brushey Fork	Noble/Keever	1		3	4
1811	Edwards, Hannah					4	2
1811	Evans, John			1			3
1811	Edwards, Benjamin			1			2
1811	Ellis, James, Jr.			1			2
1811	Ellis, James, Sr.	Licking	W. Bell	1		3	4
1811	Ellis, William			1			2
	F						
1811	Forsythe, John	Summerset	Fowler	1			4
1811	Fitzpatrick, Jas.			1			
1811	Fuller, Harrich			1			4
1811	Fulton, John	Brushey Fork		1			
1811	Fulton, Samuel		Myers				2
1811	Fryman, Henry	Beaver		1			2

Year	Person	Location & Water Course	ent/sur	(1)	(2)	(3)	(4)	
1811	Fryman, Philip	Beaver	Willing	1			4	
1811	Feeback, John			1			1	
1811	Feldies, Ebenezar	Licking	Kenton	1		1	4	
1811	Fryman, George			1			2	
1811	Fuller, Joseph			1			1	
1811	Fry, John			1			1	
1811	Fite, Jacob			1			3	
1811	Fowler, James	Ceder Creek	Henry	1			6	
1811	Fielder, George	Johnson	Johnson	1		13	7	
1811	Feelas, William			1			2	
1811	Fearman, John			1			1	
1811	(Fowler, Luke) listed in T's G	Hinkston		1		3	6	
1811	Gragg, Joseph			1			2	
1811	Glasgow, James	Beaver Creek	Logwood	1			1	
1811	Green, William			1			1	
1811	Gonsaulice, Thomas		Henry	1				
1811	Gonsaulice, James		"	1			5	
1811	Gounce, George			1			5	
1811	Griffin, Gabriel	Indian Creek	Young	1			3	
1811	Geoghegan, John	Hinkston	Haws	1			4	
1811	Gray, James						2	
1811	Griffith, Martin		Conway	1		1	3	
1811	Gaffin, Oath			1			3	
1811	Gonce, Nicholas	"	Young	1			4	
1811	Geoghegan, Michael	"	Haw	1			5	
1811	Geoghegan, John	Brushey Fork	Haw	1			3	
1811	Grosvenor, Richard	Beaver Creek	Young	1			3	
1811	Githens, John	Brushey Fork	"	1			5	
1811	Griffith, Samuel	Beaver Creek	McConnico	1		1	2	
1811	Galbreath, Benjamin	Licking	W. Bell	1			5	
1811	Githens, Henry	Brushey Fork	Haw	1			2	
1811	Gorman, Daniel			1			1	
1811	Galbreath, Daniel			1			7	
1811	Glen, Simion			1		1	2	
1811	Graham, James	Brushey Fork	Fleming	1		1	6	
1811	Gray, Isaac, Jr.			1			1	
1811	Gray, Isaac, Sr.	Cassady		1			3	
1811	Gamble, David			1			1	
1811	Gillispie, James	"	Young	1			1	
1811	Gray, David, Jr.						1	

Year	Person	Location & Water Course	ent/sur	(1)	(2)	(3)	(4)	
1811	Gulley, William			1				
1811	Gray, David, Sr.	Summerset	Fowler	1			6	
	H							
1811	How, Ezra			1			1	
1811	Hall, William	Summerset	Fowler	1			6	
1811	Hall, Moses			1				
1811	Hall, Elihu			1			1	
1811	How, Samuel	Summerset	Fowler	1			4	
1811	Hall, James	"	"	1		3	7	
1811	Howard, Jacob	Summerset	"	1			4	
1811	Hill, James	"	"	1			6	
1811	Henry, John			1			5	
1811	How, Amos			1			1	
1811	Hall, Robert	Summerset	Fowler	1		1	4	
1811	Harbert, William	Cassady	Gaither	1			2	
1811	Hartly, Mordicai			1			2	
1811	Hughes, William, Jr.			1			2	
1811	Hughes, William, Sr.			1			8	
1811	Hazlett, Samuel	Licking	Fowler	1			5	
1811	Hinton, Ezekiel	Little Flat	"	1			4	
1811	Hill, John	Cassady	"	1			6	
1811	Hall, Samuel			1		1	4	
1811	Hall, Benjamin	Cassady	Abercromby	1			6	
1811	Hawkins, Thomas			1			2	
1811	Hall, Cornelius	Brushey Fork	Haws	1		7	5	
1811	Hudson, Major			1			2	
1811	Hamilton, James			1			2	
1811	Howard, Gideon	Brushey Fork	Helms	1			3	
1811	Hanes, George			1			4	
1811	Hamilton, John	McBrides Run	Sturges	1			8	
1811	Howard, Henry	"	Fowler	1			5	
1811	Howard, Eli			1			2	
1811	Hall, Moses	Brushey Fork	Fleming	1			6	
1811	Hillock, Edward			1			1	
1811	Hillock, James			1			3	
1811	Harney, Thomas			1			1	
1811	Hollady, William	Brushey Fork	Haws	1		8	5	1s
1811	Harney, Rowland			1			3	
1811	Harney, Hiram			1			4	
1811	Harney, Mills	Beaver	Young	1			2	
1811	Heddleston, Alexander	Hinkston	Thompson	1			6	

Year	Person	Location & Water Course	ent/sur	(1)	(2)	(3)	(4)	
1811	Hardy, Armstead			1		10	4	
1811	Howerton, George			1		8	3	
1811	Huffman, Peter	Hinkston	Rece	1		1	5	
1811	Holler, John	"	Young	1			2	
1811	Holley, Thompson	"	"	1			1	
1811	Hollman, John	"		1				
1811	Hunter, James			1			2	
1811	Howard, Gideon			1			2	
1811	Hawkins, Samuel	Licking	Owings	1			4	
1811	Hildreth, Squire	"	Martin	1			5	
1811	Hunter, John			1			1	
1811	Hayse, Gabriel	Johnson	Darby	1			1	
1811	Honide, Jacob			1			2	
1811	Harden, Thomas			1		1	4	
1811	Harden, William			1			5	
1811	Hyatt, Shadrach	Little Beaver	Henry	1			2	
1811	Harden, Elihu	Licking	Binns	1		2	5	
1811	Henderson, William	Cedar Creek	Henry	-				
1811	Hill, Richard			1			1	

I

Year	Person	Location & Water Course	ent/sur	(1)	(2)	(3)	(4)	
1811	Irvin, Andrew	Hinkston	Kennady	1			6	
1811	Irvin, Samuel	R. Creek	Goodlaw	1				
1811	Irvin, George			1			3	
1811	Irvin, John			1			1	
1811	Ishmael, James			1			1	
1811	Ishmael, John			1			1	
1811	Ishmael, Thomas			1			1	

J

Year	Person	Location & Water Course	ent/sur	(1)	(2)	(3)	(4)	
1811	Johnston, James			1			1	
1811	Jenkins, Thomas	Licking	Powell	1		1	6	
1811	Juvinall, David			1			3	
1811	Jackson, John			1			2	
1811	Johnston, James	Indian Creek	Johnson	1			5	
1811	Johnston, Marion	"		1			2	
1811	Jones, Moses	Hinkston	Young	1		10	7	
1811	Johnston, William		Haws	2		1	4	
1811	Johnston, Isham	Brushey Fork	Prochtor	1		5	4	
1811	Johnston, John, Sr.			1			2	
1811	Jones, Jacob			1			2	
1811	Jones, Jacob	Brushey Fork	Haws	1			2	
1811	Jones, Drury			1			3	

Year	Person	Location & Water Course	ent/sur	(1)	(2)	(3)	(4)	
1811	Johnston, Jonathan			1			1	
1811	Jolly, Daniel	Cassady	Fowler	1			7	
	K							
1811	Kincade, George			1			1	
1811	Kincart, James	Brushey Fork	Schull	1			2	
1811	Kersin, Isabella						2	
1811	Kincart, Samuel	Brushey Fork	Fleming	1			6	
1811	Kennady, Robert	Cassady		1			3	
1811	Kilgore, William	Licking	W. Bell	1			3	
1811	Kennady, Andrew			1			2	
1811	Kennady, David	Brushey Fork	Moore	1			4	
1811	Kincart, John		Claytor	1			2	
1811	Kimbrough, Elizabeth	Hinkston	D. Rice				2	
1811	Kiles, John			1			5	
1811	Kimbrough, Robert H.	"	Young	1		1	2	
1811	Kimbrough, John		"	1		6	3	
1811	(Kimbrough, Susanna) listed under Moses Jones							
1811	Kreeson, Michael	Johnson	Darby	1			3	
1811	Keith, Philip	Ceder Creek	Henry	1			8	
1811	Keith, Jacob	Little Beaver	"	1			4	
1811	Keith, Adam		Monro	1			5	
1811	Kelly, Thomas			1			2	
	L							
1811	Louderback, Anderson	Ceder Creek	Henry	1			5	
1811	Logan, David	Johnson		1			4	
1811	Lowe, George	Indian Creek	Young	1			6	
1811	Lilly, Pleasant			1		1	7	
1811	Livingood, George	Beaver Creek		1			2	
1811	Lockridge, Robert	Licking	Willing	1			2	
1811	Lockridge, William	Summerset	W. Bell	1			3	
1811	Lockridge, James		Fowler	1			6	
1811	Lockridge, John	Summerset	Fowler	3			6	
1811	Leeper, John	"	Homes	1		1	10	
1811	Low, Isaac	Licking	Fowler	1			6	
	M							
1811	McCall, James			1			3	
1811	Mannon, Samuel			1			7	
1811	Mannon, Meredith			1			5	
1811	Mannon, John			1			2	
1811	Moler, Isaac	Summerset	Dapuy	1			7	
1811	Murphy, Zephariah	"		1			7	

Year	Person	Location & Water Course	ent/sur	(1)	(2)	(3)	(4)
1811	Myers, Christian			1			1
1811	McDowell, Margaret	Summerset	Abercromby				11
1811	McLean, Charles		"	1			4
1811	Marshall, David	"	Fowler	1			3
1811	McAnully, Joseph		"	1			5
1811	McCoy, David		"	1			2
1811	Morris, Thomas		"	1			1
1811	McAnually, James	"		1			2
1811	Miller, James			1			2
1811	McLees, William	Cassady	"	1			3
1811	McMahan, Robert	Summerset	"	1		2	9
1811	McCoy, Andrew	Cassady		1			3
1811	McDonald, Mordicai			1			2
1811	McAnully, John			1			1
1811	Myers, John	Licking		1		1	7
1811	McCall, John		W. Bell	1			
1811	Marshall, Archibald	Licking	W. Bell	1		2	10
1811	McClanigan, James		Fowler	1		1	3
1811	Morris, John			1		1	2
1811	Morgan, Joseph			1			2
1811	Myers, Margaret	Cassady					4
1811	Myers, Abraham			1			1
1811	Myers, Henry			1			3
1811	Myers, Daniel						2
1811	McQuoin, Lawrence	Licking	W. Bell	1			2
1811	Myers, David	"		1			
1811	McDonald, Joseph	"	Gather	1			3
1811	McDonald, John			1			3
1811	Myers, Lewis			1			1
1811	McDonald, George	"	W. Bell	1			1
1811	Morgan, Garrard	"	Young	1			9
1811	Myers, George			1			
1811	McDonald, Alexander	"	W. Bell	1			2
1811	McClanigan, William			1			
1811	Moore, Samuel, Sr.			1			2
1811	Moore, Samuel, Jr.						1
1811	McCune, Robert, Sr.	McBrides Run	Swearingen	1			5
1811	McCormack, Adam	Brushey Fork	Keever	1		2	4
1811	McDowell, James			1			
1811	McLaughlin, John			1			2
1811	Marsh, Thomas	"	Bullard	1		8	10

Year	Person	Location & Water Course	ent/sur	(1)	(2)	(3)	(4)
1811	Myers, Christian			1			1
1811	Morgan, Agnes	Row Run					1
1811	McMihill, Thomas		A. Noble	1			2
1811	McDowell, William	Brushey Fork	F. Rece	2		1	7
1811	(McDowell, James) added into William McDowell						
1811	Maxwell, William	Brushey Fork	Sturgess	1			4
1811	McCune, Gavin			1			2
1811	Mitchell, Joseph			1		1	2
1811	McMihill, John	Brushey Fork	Fleming	1			2
1811	McCune, John	McBrides Run	Swearingen	1			4
1811	Mitchell, Ezekiel			1			1
1811	Mathers, William	Brushey Fork	Fleming	1			6
1811	Mathers, James			1			4
1811	McCune, Robert			1			6
1811	McLaughlin, William			1			2
1811	Mathers, John						1
1811	Maxwell, Gavin			1			2
1811	Mathers, Gavin			1			4
1811	Mitcheltree, John			1			1
1811	Man, Peter	Brushey Fork	Ingram	1			5
1811	McLaughlin, John			1			
1811	Maynard, Jeremiah	Beaver	McConico	1			2
1811	McCormack, James			1			2
1811	McCormack, Widdow	Brushey Fork	Young				3
1811	Marshall, Samuel	Beaver	McConnico	1			4
1811	Man, John	Brushey Fork	Ingram	1			6
1811	Morris, Morris			1			1
1811	Miller, Abraham, Sr.	Indian Creek	Young	1			4
1811	Miller, Abraham, Jr.			1			2
1811	McShain, Daniel	Indian Creek	"	3			5
1811	McClintock, Hugh	Hinkston	Frabue	2			10
1811	Maffett, Henry	Indian Creek	Young	1			3
1811	Marshall, Hugh	Beaver	Goodlaw	1			4
1811	McClintock, Joseph	Hinkston	Thompson	1			4
1811	Monson, Joel			1			3
1811	Mullen, Samuel			1			
1811	McClintock, Thomas			1			2
1811	Maffett, Thomas	Hinkston	Young	1		2	4
1811	Maffett, William			1		1	5
1811	McFarland, William	Indian Creek	Johnson	2			5
1811	Marshall, William			1			1

Year	Person	Location & Water Course	ent/sur	(1)	(2)	(3)	(4)	
1811	McClintock, William			1			2	
1811	Murphy, W. George	Hinkston	Cook	1			5	
1811	Monicle, Christopher			1			6	
1811	Monicle, Peter			1			3	
1811	Maffett, Mathew			1			1	
1811	Metcalf, Eli	Johnson	Walden	2		5	2	
1811	McCord, John	Elk Creek	Darby	1			3	1s
1811	McCarty, Thomas	Buchanan	Darby	1			2	
1811	Martin, John	Licking	Johnson	1			7	
1811	Martin, James			1			3	
1811	McCord, David	Johnson	Darby	1			4	
1811	McCabe, Josiah	Elk Creek	Darby	1		3	2	
1811	Martin, Nehemiah	Johnson	Johnson	1			4	
1811	McCord, Michael			1				
1811	McCarty, Felix			1				
1811	McCord, William, Sr.	Johnson	Darby	1			2	
1811	McClurg, Joseph	Elk Creek	Darby	1			4	
1811	Morgan, Charles			1			3	
1811	McCarty, David, Sr.			1				
1811	McCarty, James			1			1	
1811	Mason, Benjamin	Ceder Creek	Metcalf	1		1	2	
1811	Menach, Alexander			1				
1811	McMehan, Archibald	"	Henry	1			2	
1811	Metcalf, Thomas	Ceder Creek	Metcalf	1		9	4	
1811	McGuire, John			1			1	
1811	Mason, Burgess	Ceder Creek	Metcalf	1		8	5	
	N							
1811	Nudigate, John			1			4	
1811	Neaves, Walter			1			1	
1811	Neaves, Daniel			1			1	
1811	Nudigate, William	Johnson	Thornton	1			4	
1811	Nesbit, Nathan	Brushey Fork	Fleming	1			6	
1811	Nesbit, Thomas	"	Fleming	1			5	
1811	Nichol, Robert			1			1	
1811	Nelson, Moses			1			3	
	O							
1811	Olfrey, James			1			5	
1811	Overfield, Moses	Johnson	Johnson	1			2	
1811	Olliver, John	Ceder Creek	Henry	1			5	
1811	Overby, Henry	Johnson	Kenton	1		3	6	
	P							

Year	Person	Location & Water Course	ent/sur	(1)	(2)	(3)	(4)	
1811	Pursley, Thomas	Ceder Creek	Metcalf	1			3	
1811	Porvel, George	Ceder Creek	Metcalf	1			2	
1811	Pritchett, William	Preston Run	Henry	1		6	4	
1811	Prater, Ashford			1			2	
1811	Prater, William			1			1	
1811	Prater, Jeremiah, Sr.	Elk Creek	Darby	1		2	6	
1811	Prater, Jeremiah			1				
1811	Parkes, James			1			1	
1811	Philips, John			1				
1811	Peyton, Samuel			1			3	
1811	Purnel, William	Beaver	Welling	1		2	4	
1811	Peyton, Stephen			1			3	
1811	Peyton, Stephen, Sr.	Brushey Fork	Logan	1			5	
1811	Powel, Jeremiah	"	Power	1			6	
1811	Peyton, Thomas			2			4	
1811	Paxton, Robert	"	Fowler	1			8	
1811	Potts, William	Summerset	Fowler	1		8	6	
1811	Parsons, John			1			6	1s
1811	Poe, William	"	Fowler	1			1	
1811	Plew, Jeremiah			1			1	
1811	Plew, Philip			1			2	
1811	Powel, Zenas	"	Cox	1			7	
1811	Pauley, Abraham			1			1	
1811	Powel, Jeremiah			1			4	
1811	Powel, Charles	Flat Creek	Fowelly	1			5	
1811	Powel, John			1			5	
1811	Powel, Thomas, Sr.	Summerset	Abercromby	1			13	
1811	Pauley, John			1			4	
1811	Pauley, William	"	Cox	1			1	
1811	Pendergrass, Edward			1			5	
1811	Powel, Thomas, Jr.	Flat Creek	Fowler	1			4	
1811	Powel, Isaac			1			2	
1811	Paget, Daniel			1			2	
	R							
1811	Roberts, John			1		1	6	
1811	Rice, Jany			1				
1811	Richard, William	Flat Creek	Homer	1			5	
1811	Reding, William			1			3	
1811	Randal, Richard	Licking	Fowler	1			4	
1811	Roberts, Thomas			1			3	
1811	Robertson, Samuel			2			8	

Year	Person	Location & Water Course	ent/sur	(1)	(2)	(3)	(4)	
1811	Reding, Eli	Summerset	Fowler	1			2	
1811	Roberts, Henly	"	Fowler	1			3	
1811	Ramsey, Archibald			1			1	
1811	Rodes, Beecham	Licking	Gaither	1			4	
1811	Roades, Silas	"		1			4	
1811	Revral, Thomas	"		1			4	
1811	Riley, John	Cassady	Fowler	1			8	
1811	Roberts, Nehemiah			1			1	
1811	Robertson, James	Brushey Fork	Helms	1		2	4	
1811	Ray, Francis	"	Stockton	2			10	
1811	Robertson, Alexander	"	Helms	1			4	
1811	Reveal, Joseph	"	Myers	1			5	
1811	Richey, Noah	Beaver	Young	1			3	
1811	Richey, Esau	Beaver Creek	Young	1			2	
1811	Richey, Solomon	"	"	1			2	
1811	Richey, Isaac	"	"	1			2	
1811	Reveal, Michael	Brushey Fork	Claytor	1			2	
1811	Ross, Alexander			1			3	
1811	Richey, Gilbert			1			2	
1811	Richey, Robert	Hinkston	Cook	1			6	
1811	Rankins, Moses	Martins Run	Johnson	1			4	
1811	Robb, William			1				
1811	Retzatt, Peter			1				

S

Year	Person	Location & Water Course	ent/sur	(1)	(2)	(3)	(4)	
1811	Stewart, Willoughby	Seder Creek	(Hisery)	1			4	
1811	Sater, John			1				
1811	Sloop, Joseph	North Fork	Thornton	1			3	
1811	Stewart, James			1			6	
1811	Stogdale, James, Sr.			1			3	
1811	Spaw, Henry			1		1	12	
1811	Stogdale, William			1			3	
1811	Standiford, George			1				
1811	Standiford, James			1			1	
1811	Standiford, John	Licking	Martin	1			3	
1811	Spaws, Jacob			1			1	
1811	Swain, Nathaniel	Buchanan	Mosely	1			4	
1811	Smith, William	Johnson	Thornton	1			8	
1811	Smith, John	Johnson		1		1	4	
1811	Standeford, Aquilla	Hinkston	Haws	1			4	1s
1811	Satterfield, Clemment			1			2	
1811	Summerset, Christian	"		1			6	

Year	Person	Location & Water Course	ent/sur	(1)	(2)	(3)	(4)	
1811	Snap, Daniel			1			2	
1811	Sadler, Edward			1			1	
1811	Summerset, George			2			7	
1811	Snap, George	Hinkston	Cook	1			3	
1811	Snap, John			1		1	1	
1811	Sadler, John		Haws	1			3	
1811	Stewart, Joseph	Indian Creek	Young	1			6	
1811	Sharp, T. John			1			4	
1811	Smith, James	Beaver	Goodloe	1			1	
1811	Stewart, Mary	Hinkston	Rice				2	
1811	Snap, Peter	"	Cook	1			3	
1811	Snap, Samuel			1			2	
1811	Stephenson, Thomas	"	Young	2		1	15	
1811	Scott, Thomas	Indian Creek	Young	1			6	
1811	Scott, Mathew	"	Young	1		1	7	
1811	Short, George			1			1	
1811	Smith, Mitchell			1			3	
1811	Steel, Joseph			1			3	
1811	Steel, Hugh			1			3	
1811	Saunders, Hezekiah			1			2	
1811	Selby, Isaac			1			2	
1811	Stears, William			1			2	
1811	Stockwell, John	Brushey Fork	Young	1			15	
1811	Stears, John			1		2	6	
1811	Stears, James			1				
1811	Shanklin, David			1			1	
1811	Smaly, John			1			2	1s
1811	Stoops, Philip	Cassady	Gaithens	1			4	
1811	Scott, Andrew	"	"	1			4	
1811	Saunderson, John	Licking	Young	1			5	
1811	Scott, Thomas	Cassady	Fowler	1			3	
1811	Shanklin, John	"	Gaithens	1			4	
1811	Smart, Humphrey			1			1	
1811	Stephenson, Robert, Sr.	"	Fowler	1			5	
1811	Smith, Abraham			1			2	
1811	Stephenson, Robert, Jr.	Little Flat	Fowler	1			4	
1811	Stephenson, Joseph	"	"	1			3	
1811	Summerset, Richard	Licking	"	1			4	
1811	Smith, Job			1				
1811	Smith, David	Summerset	"	1			4	
1811	Smith, John	"	"	1			2	

Year	Person	Location & Water Course	ent/sur	(1)	(2)	(3)	(4)	
1811	Stephenson, William	"	"	1			6	
1811	Saunders, James	Summerset	Fowler	1			5	
1811	Scott, John	"	"	1			3	
1811	Stephenson, Betsy						6	
1811	Shannon, Margaret	"	"				3	
1811	Shannon, Samuel	"	"	1				
1811	Smith, Hezekiah			1			7	
	T							
1811	Thomson, James	Cassady	Fowler	1			2	
1811	Thomson, William	Summerset	"	1			9	
1811	Thomson, Susannah	Cassady	"				5	
1811	Thomson, H. James	Summerset	"	2			6	
1811	Thompson, Samuel	Cassady	"	1			1	
1811	Tarvar, George			1			2	
1811	Thompson, Sally					3	3	
1811	Taylor, George	Beaver	Willing	1			3	
1811	Thomas, Edward	Brushey Fork	Moore	1			3	
1811	Thompson, Daniel	Hinkston	Thompson	1		2	5	
1811	Taylor, George			1			2	
1811	Thompson, Henry, Sr.	Hinkston	Thompson	2		2	11	
1811	Taylor, Joshua			1		2	3	
1811	(Fowler, Luke)	Hinkston	Goodlow	1		3	6	
1811	Thornton, Anthony	Johnson	Thornton	1		34	7	
1811	Truelove, C. William	Johnson	Moseby	1			3	
1811	Taylor, Nathaniel			1			2	
1811	Taylor, Tapley	Ceder Creek	Henry	1			1	
1811	Throckmorton, Ariss			1		3	8	
1811	Taylor, John, Sr.	Brinsons Run	Henry	1			3	
1811	Taylor, John, Jr.			1			1	
1811	Throckmorton, Thomas, Jr.	Licking	Taylor	1		6	7	
1811	Throckmorton, John	Johnson	Kenton	1		6	8	
1811	Throckmorton. Thomas, Sr.	Licking	Throckmort	1		14	10	
	U							
1811	Ureglis, John	Licking	Henry	1		2	2	
	V							
1811	Venoy, Francis	Johnson	Montgomery	1		2	4	
1811	Verden, Hugh			1			3	
1811	Vanhook, Abner	Indian Creek	Johnson	1			4	
1811	Vanhook, Archelaus	"	"	1			2	
1811	Vanhook, Samuel			1			1	
1811	Vaughan, Thomas	Licking	Durham	1		4	11	

Year	Person	Location & Water Course	ent/sur	(1)	(2)	(3)	(4)	
1811	Vansdike, Hezekiah W	Summerset	Abercromby	1			8	
1811	Wiley, John, Jr.			1			4	
1811	Wiley, Hugh	Flat Creek	Fowler	1			3	
1811	Wiley, William			1			5	
1811	Wiley, John, Sr.			1			5	
1811	Wiley, Samuel			1			4	
1811	Wiley, Robert			1			1	
1811	Wilson, Charles	Summerset	Abercromby	1			7	
1811	Weaver, Abraham			1			1	
1811	William, John	Summerset	Fowler	1			3	1s
1811	Warrant, Isaac			1			2	
1811	West, Philip			1			1	
1811	Wells, John	Cassady		1			4	
1811	Wheeler, William			1			5	
1811	West, Isaac	"	Gaithins	1			9	
1811	Williams, William			1			1	
1811	Waugh, M. Samuel	Brushey Fork	Fowler	1		1	6	
1811	Wilson, Isaac			1			4	
1811	West, Amos	McBrisdes Run	(Berry)	1		4	11	1s
1811	Wilson, Benjamin	Brushey Fork	Young	1			3	
1811	West, Elijah			1				
1811	Wood, Hilkiah					2	2	
1811	Webster, Nathaniel			1			1	
1811	Waterford, Benjamin			1			2	
1811	Waggoner, John			1			6	
1811	Waggoner, Christian			1			4	
1811	Wrights, Charles						2	
1811	Williamson, John			1			1	
1811	West, John			1			4	
1811	Wrights, John	Indian Creek	Young	1			6	1s
1811	Woollen, Leonard	"	Johnson	1			3	
1811	West, Thomas			1			2	
1811	Whitely, William			1			1	
1811	Webb, Charles	Hinkston	Young	1			3	
1811	White, John			1			3	
1811	Whitaker, James	Buchanan	Mosely	1		1	3	
1811	Wiggins, John	Licking		1		2	7	
1811	Wells, Aaron	Johnson	Johnson	1			5	
1811	Wiggins, William			1			3	
1811	Waugh, Jacob	Buchanan	Darby	1			9	

64

Year	Person	Location & Water Course	ent/sur	(1)	(2)	(3)	(4)	
1811	Woolums, William			1			2	
1811	Wilson, John			1			2	
1811	William, William			1			2	
1811	Wallace, William	Johnson		1		2	7	
1811	Watson, Patrick	Licking	Monro	1			6	
1811	Whitely, David			1			3	
1811	Watson, James	Beaver	Monro	1			6	
1811	Wilson, Robert			1				
1811	Wells, Nathan			1			2	
1811	Wilson, James	Ceder Creek	Henry	1			6	
1811	West, Thomas	Johnson	Johnson	1			8	
	Y							
1811	Young, Alexander			1			1	
1811	Young, Jacob			1			8	
1811	Yates, Andrew	Summerset	Dupree	1		1	3	

End 1811

NICHOLAS COUNTY, KENTUCKY

TAX LISTS

1800-1811

NOTES:

It appears there were 2 lists taken annually. Not all the dual lists have survived and the reader can quickly locate those years with only one list. 1804 & 1805 show two commissioners and two separate lists. Others years begin the list with "added." One list says commissioner for District 2, but it does not appear the county was divided, instead it looks like everyone who paid on time was on one list and all the others on a second list.

The lists were recorded semi-alphabetically. Example: all A's together, but not in order. Please check box to right for different spellings. The name to the left is the commonly used spelling in other county records. (Sometimes the clerk's hand-writting or the ink made translation difficult and the spelling is what I read not what the clerk wrote. For example in 1807 Mc was recorded MC with a lower case letter for the rest of the name. MCdannal becomes McDonald [and it still looks like Mcrenal]. Elimination and four opinions make it McDannal - an earlier spelling in the lists).

It is likely that the tax commissioner was appointed for two years. There was also an examiner and sometimes the county clerk was listed.

COMMISSIONERS

EXAMINERS

1800-1801 - James Parks
1802-1803 - John Allison
1804-1805 - Michael Geoghegan (Dist. # 2) see 1808
        and
    David Ballingal (Probably #1 as in 1807)
   These lists also have date tax taken.
1806 -   - Jesse Basket (very poorly done)
      Mc - names appear under other part of name
      McClintock listed in C for Clintock, but with Mc.
      Some name out of alphabetic order.
1807 -   - Archelaus Van Hook
1808 -   - Jesse Basket
-------   no other commissioners recorded

1800-1804 Lewis H. Arnold
1805-1811 Joseph Morgan

The 1809 list has both tax lists, the second recorded "revised." The revised list is very in poor condition as seen in the first section of this book where blanks have been used for illegible names.The entire 1810 list is a very poor copy. Water stains and poor quality ink make many of the names illegible when reading microfilm.

For that reason the 1810 tax list has been compared with the 1810 census and because of the poor quality of 1810, 1811 was also abstracted. The result is actually an enlarged census and "proof" that many people were missed on the census rolls. The third section of the book shows the 1809 - 1810 -1811 lists. Please notice how many long time residents where not enmerated in the 1810 census. Also long a the number of one time tax entries who were listed on the 1810 census. These could only have been travelers who stopped long enough to be tallied in the census.

NOTE:
Surames are listed first follwed by the given name. However, if there was a middle name or initial, the names are "completely" reversed on original. Example: John A. Smith appears: Smith, A. John. Comparison of others records and signatures verify this point.

It is possible that the duplicated names in any one year represent the same person, but the commissioners usually list duplicate tax entries for the same person directly under that name and use ditto marks. (0a -9a etc. means more that one entry for that name and in that year.

These lists were read at separte times and recorded as a first impression. After all lists were compiled, as attempt was make to locate duplicated names.

(0a) duplicate in same year

Person	18	00	01	02	03	04	05	06	07	08	09	10	11	
09 A's - unknown 3											x			
01 Abner, William			x											
09 Abraham, (Moriseth)											x			
04 Adams, Hannah						x								
Adams, Ralph		x	x	x	x									
Adams, Thomas		x	x	x										
Adams, William		x	x	x	x									
02 Alb-----h, -xanpe (?)				x										
04 Alexander, Jesse						x	x	x		x	x	x		
10 Alexander, Thomas												x	x	
02 Allen, James				x										
08, Allen, John										x				
Allen, William		x	x	x	x		x	x			x	x	x	
05 Allen, William, Jr.							x	x			x	x		
04 Allfrey, James						x	x	x		x		x		
Allison, Alexander		x	x	x	x		x		x		x	x	x	2-Alb---h, xanpe
Allison, John		x	x	x	x	x	x		x		x	x	x	
03 Airs, John					x									
03 Airs, Thomas					x									
02 Anders, James (?)				x										
03 Anderson, Daniel					x	x	x	x		x		x	x	
10 Anderson, Edward												x	x	
Anderson, George		x	x	x	x	x	x	x		x	x	x	x	8-Sr.
05, Anderson, George, Jr.							x			x				
Anderson, James		x	x	x	x	x		x		x	x			
11 Anderson, Jesse													x	
Anderson, John		x	x	x	x						x	x	x	
10 Anderson, Richard												x		
10 Anderson, Sarah												x	x	
02 Archer, James				x	x	x		x		x		x	x	
Archer, John		x	x	x	x	x	x	x		x	x	x	x	5-Sr.
04 Archer, John						x	x	x		x	x	x	x	5-Jr.
02 Archer, Sampson				x	x	x		x		x	x	x	x	
Ardery, James		x	x		x	x	x	x		x		x	x	
09 Ardery, Robert											x	x	x	
02 Arelywine														see Earlywine
10 Armstrong, Irvin												x	x	
03 Armstrong, William					x									
Arnett, Samuel		x	x		x	x	x	x		x	x	x	x	0-ot 5Arneth 6Arnet

Person	18	00	01	02	03	04	05	06	07	08	09	10	11
Arnold, Lewis H.		x	x	x	x	x	x					x	x
10 Artt, James												x	x
01 Art, Robert			x	x	x								
02 Art, Thomas				x	x							x	x
Art, William		x	x	x	x	x	x		x		x	x	x
01 Art, William, Jr.			x	x		x					x	x	x
07 Asberry, Henry									x		x	x	x
03 Asberry, William					x	x	x		x		x	x	x
03 Asberry, William, Jr.					x	x	x		x		x	x	x
05 Ashbrook, Henry							x						
07, Ashbrook, Thomas									x		x		
02 Ashcraft,Ephraim				x	x	x	x			x	x	x	x
Ashcraft, Jacob		x	x	x	x	x	x				x	x	x
10 Ashley, James												x	x
Atkins, John		x											

70

Person	1800	01	02	03	04	05	06	07	08	09	10	11	
09 B's - unknown 6 in census	- 8	by	me										
01 Bailey, Basel		x	x	x	x	x		x		x	x	x	3-Bayley 10 Baley
11 Bailey, Benedict													x	
Bailey, John	x	x	x	x	x	x	x		x		x			6-Bayley
08 Baker, Jacob									x		x	x		
Baker, James	x	x						x		x	x	x		
07 Baker, James (7a)								x						
07 Baker, John								x		x	x	x		
09 Baker, John (9a)										x	x			
Baker, Martin	x	x	x	x	x					x	x	x		
Baker, Martin, Jr.	x				x									
Baker, William	x	x	x	x	x	x		x			x	x		
09 Ball, James										x				
Ballingall, David	x	x	x	x	x	x		x		x	x	x		7-Benin' 9Bedin'
10 Ballenger, William											x	x		
09 Barlow, David										x				
03 Barlow, Eliphet			x	x	x	x		x						
04 Barlow, Jesse				x	x	x		x			x	x		
Barlow, John	x	x		x	x	x	x		x	x	x	x		10 Barwell
11 Barlow, John (11a)													x	
Barlow, Thomas	x	x		x	x	x	x		x					
Barlow, William	x	x	x	x	x	x	x		x	x	x	x		
09 Barnes, John										x				
Barnet, Ambrose	x	x	x	x	x	x	x		x	x	x	x		
01 Barnet, James		x												
05 Barnet, John					x	x		x		x	x	x		
05 Barnet, William					x	x		x		x	x	x		5/7/10-Burnet
10 Bartlett, (Cenna)										x				
Bartlett, Ebenzer	x	x	x	x		x		x		x	x	x		
09 Bartlett, Joseph										x	x	x		
Bartlett, Samuel	x	x	x	x		x				x	x	x		
Bartlett, William	x	x	x	x	x	x		x		x	x	x		
Basket, Jesse	x	x	x	x	x	x	x		x	x	x	x		
10 Barwell, John										x				
04 Beach, John				x	x									5-Beachy
04 Bear, David				x										
01 Beard, George		x	x	x	x									3-Baird
Beard, John	x	x	x	x	x	x								3-Baird
Beard, John (0a)	x	x		x	x									3-Baird
06 Beard, Mary							x		x					
Beard, William	x													

Person	18 00	01	02	03	04	05	06	07	08	09	10	11	
Beater/Beaton													see Beaty
03 Beaty, John			x	x	x						x	x	5-Beasnt 10'ton 11'ter
04 Beaty, John (4a)				x									
07 Beatty, Michael							x						
02 Beaver, John			x										(Beaty ?)
06 Becher, Jacob						x							
Bedinger, George M.	x	x	x	x			x				x	x	
05 Bedinger, Philip					x	x							
Bell, Adam	x												
03 Bell, Jane			x	x	x	x					x	x	
10 Bell, Jane (10a)											x	x	
05 Bell, James					x		x		x				
Bell, John	x	x	x	x	x	x	x		x				9-Beall
Bell, Robert	x	x	x										
01 Bell, William		x											
Bennington, Nehemiah	x	x	x	x	x	x	x		x	x		x	
10 Bennington, William										x			
Benson, James	x	x											
Benson, John	x	x											
11 Bentley, James												x	
Bentley, Michael	x	x	x	x		x					x	x	
11 (Bentred), Josiah												x	
Berry, John	x												
Berry, Robert	x		x	x	x	x	x		x		x	x	
09 (Biles), John										x			
11 Bishop, Teril												x	
Black, Richard	x												
10 Blackburn, Julius H.											x	x	
Blackburn, William	x	x	x										
Blair, Alexander	x	x	x	x		x	x		x		x	x	
02 Blair, Alex. (exec.)			x										
05 Blair, John						x	x						5-(Blain)
10 Blair, Sarah											x		
05 Blanchard, Laban						x							
10 Blastengun, William											x		
02 Blunt, Reading			x	x		x	x					x	11-Blount
Boatman, Henry	x	x						x	x	x	x		9-Boteman
01 Boatman, William		x											
03 Bogges, Thomas			x	x	x		x		x	x	x		3-Bogus
06 Bolders, Thomas							x						
09 Boles, John						x		x	x	x	x		5-Bowles 9-Bales

Person	1800	01	02	03	04	05	06	07	08	09	10	11	
Bolen, William	x	x		x	x						x	x	3- Bowlin 10-Boles
Boon, Abner	x	x	x	x									
Boon, Jacob	x	x											
02 Boon, Joab			x										
01 Bosby, William		x											
03 Bossley, Bennidick				x	x	x	x		x		x		10 Benax
10 Boswell, William											x		
08 Boulden, Thomas									x				
Bowen, William	x		x	x		x			x	x	x	x	
Bowles/Bowlin													see Boles
05 Boyd, Ally						x	x						6-Ayley Boid
Boyd, John	x	x	x	x	x	x	x		x		x	x	6-Boid
10 Boyd, John (10a)											x		
Boyd, William	x	x	x	x	x								
06 Brachey, Robert							x						
02 Bradford, John			x										
07 Bradly, Daniel								x			x		
11 Bradley, David												x	
09 Brady, Elisha										x			
07 Bradly, George								x		x	x	x	9-Brady
09 Bradly, Robert										x	x	x	
05 Bradley, Susannah						x							
09 Bradshaw, David										x	x	x	
08 Bradshaw, Robert									x				
11 Bradshaw, William												x	
10 Branen, James											x		10 Broren
09 Branon, John										x	x		
09 Branon, Thomas										x			
02 Bratton, Joseph			x	x	x	x							2-Soshva (?) 5-Joshua
04 Bratton, Robert					x	x	x						
01 Bright, Hanson		x	x	x									
03 Bright, William				x		x	x						
10 Brinton, Eliza											x		
10 Brinton, James											x	x	
10 Brinson, John											x		
Brinson, Jonathan	x			x						x	x	x	3-Brunson 9 Brinton
05 Brinton, Robert						x				x		x	9-Brinton 11 Brenton
Brinson, Thomas	x	x	x	x	x	x			x	x	x	x	3-Brunson 11-Sr.
11 Brinson, Thomas, Jr.												x	
09 Brooks, Susanna										x	x		10-Hannah
07 Brooks, William								x					

Person	18 00	01	02	03	04	05	06	07	08	09	10	11	
08 Brooks, Zachariah									x		x	x	
03 Brown, Allexander			x	x	x				x	x		x	
02 Brown, David			x	x	x	x	x		x			x	11-Sr.
09 Brown, Ja---										x			
Brown, James	x	x	x	x	x				x	x	x	x	
03 Brown, James (3a)				x	x				x	x			
Brown, John	x	x		x	x	x	x	x	x		x	x	
03 Brown, John (3a)				x	x	x	x		x		x	x	
09 Brown, John (9a)										x		x	
11 Brown, Jursey												x	
09 Brown, H---										x			
05 Brown, Parker						x					x	x	5-Larkin
08, Brown, William									x		x	x	
02 Bryant, Samuel			x	x									
Buchannan, James	x	x	x	x	x	x							
02 Buchannon, Jonathan			x										
07 Buchannon, Phebe								x		x	x	x	
05 Buchannon, William						x							
09 Buckler, Robert										x		x	
02 Bucklor, Stephen			x	x							x	x	
06 Buckner, Henry							x		x		x	x	11-Harry
09 Buckner, James										x			
Buckner, Phillip	x												
Buckner, Robert	x	x	x	x	x	x							
03 Buckner, Samuel			x	x	x	x			x		x	x	
08 Bunton, Andrew									x		x	x	
10 Bunton, Charles											x	x	
02 Bunton, James	x	x	x	x	x	x	x		x		x	x	0/1-Benton
06 Bunton, James (6a)							x						
02 Bunton, John	x	x	x	x	x	x	x		x		x		0/1-Benton
10 Bunton, Josiah											x		
08 Bunton, Robert									x				
02 Bunton, William	x	x	x	x	x	x	x		x		x	x	01/-Benton
01 Burden, Benjamin		x	x	x		x	x						3-Birdon
Burden, James	x	x	x	x	x	x							3-Birdon
Burden, John	x	x			x								
05 Burden, John (5a)						x							
Burnett													see Barnett
11 Burns, Mathew												x	
11 Burris, James												x	
02 Burns, John			x	x				x			x		

Person	18	00	01	02	03	04	05	06	07	08	09	10	11	
02 Burius, John				x		x	x	x					x	5-Burrus
02 Burrius, John				x			x				x		x	x	8 Burrows
11 Burris, John (11a)														x	
05 Burris, William							x								
Burwell, Ephraim		x													
09 Busby, Archibald												x		x	
10 Busby, Mathew													x	x	
02 Busby, William				x	x	x	x					x	x	x	3-Bazby
Byers, David		x	x	x	x	x	x	x			x		x	x	
10 Byers, John													x	x	
08 Byrum, Agustus											x	x	x	x	9-Bryam
11 Byram, Valentine														x	

Person	18	00	01	02	03	04	05	06	07	08	09	10	11	
09 C's - 15 unknown														
09 Cack, David											x			
Caldwell, Alexander		x	x	x	x	x	x	x		x		x	x	
Caldwell, David		x	x	x	x	x	x	x		x	x	x	x	6-Sr.
Caldwell, David (0a)		x	x	x		x	x	x		x		x	x	
02 Caldwell, James				x										
Caldwell, Robert		x	x	x	x	x	x	x		x	x	x	x	
02 Caldwell, Robert (2a)			x		x	x	x					x	x	
Caldwell, Robert, Jr.		x		x	x					x			x	
03 Caldwell, Thomas				x	x	x	x			x	x	x	x	
10 Caldwell, Thomas (10a)												x		
05 Caldwell, Walter							x	x		x	x	x		
Caldwell, William		x	x	x	x	x	x	x	x	x		x	x	7-McCadwell
Caldwell, William (0a)		x	x	x	x	x	x					x		
02 Caldwell, William (2a)				x		x								
07 Caha, John									x		x			
10 Camerett, George											x			
Cameron, John		x	x	x	x		x							
Cameron, John (0a)		x												
Cameron, Samuel		x	x	x	x	x	x		x				x	
10 Campbell, Daniel											x	x		
Campbell, David		x	x											0/1-Campble
Campbell, James		x	x	x	x	x	x	x		x	x		x	0/1-Campble
Campbell, James(0a)		x	x	x										
01 Campbel, Jas. (1a)			x											
04 Campbell, John					x		x				x	x		
Campbell, Jossias		x	x	x	x	x		x		x		x	x	0/1Campble 11Jonas
11 Campbell, Robert													x	
10 Campbell, Samuel											x			
Campble, William		x	x											
Campble, William(0a)		x												
Canady														see Kennedy
Carbough, Jacob		x	x		x									
04 Carabough, Peter					x	x		x			x			6-Carrabough
Carothers, Thomas		x	x	x	x	x	x		x		x	x	x	9-Carthers
11 Carrothers, Gabriel													x	
08 Carnaham, Aaron										x				
03 Carnahan, James				x		x	x			x	x	x	x	6-Sr.
03 Carnahan, James (3a)				x			x			x	x	x	x	6-Jr.
03 Carnahan, John				x	x	x	x							6-K
03 Carnahan, Joseph				x	x	x	x							6-K

Person	00	01	02	03	04	05	06	07	08	09	10	11	
04 Carnahan, Robert					x	x	x		x	x	x	x	
Carns													see Kerns
02 Carrence, Adam			x		x								
09 Carter, Daniel										x	x	x	
08 Carter, John									x				
01 Carter, Jonathan		x								x	x		
08 Carter, Joseph									x				
Carver, (no name)	x												
03 Carey, William				x									(Casey ?)
01 Carswell, Petter Edward		x		x	x	x							1-Carpoell, Ed. P.
Casey, James	x		x	x			x			x	x		9-Kasey10Casesey
08 Casey, John									x		x	x	10-Casesey
07 Cash, Benjamin								x					
09 Cassabaugh, Ester										x			
Cassidy, Daniel	x	x	x	x	x	x	x		x	x	x	x	
01 Cassady, James		x	x	x	x	x	x		x	x	x	x	
03 Cassady, James (3a)				x						x			
08 Cassady, Jeremiah									x	x			
05 Cassida, Thomas						x			x				
03 Cassidy, William				x	x		x		x				
Catherwood, Charles	x	x	x	x		x		x		x		x	7/9-Ketherwood
10 Catherwood, John											x		
Catherwood, Samuel	x		x	x	x	x	x		x	x	x		7/9-Ketherwood
10 Caughey, David										x	x		
Caughey, John	x	x	x	x	x	x	x			x	x		
06 Caven, H. William							x						
10 Chaney, James										x	x		
08 Chaney, John									x		x		
10 Chaney, John (10a)											x		
06 Chaney, Leonard							x						
06 Chaney, William							x		x		x	x	
03 Chipley, Edward				x									
Chipman, Draper	x	x		x									0-Drake
09 Claney, James										x			
09 Claney, William										x			
03 Clarke, Allexander				x	x	x							
09 Clark, Benjamin										x	x	x	
10 Clark, Benjamin (10a)											x	x	
04 Clarke, David					x	x	x	x		x	x		
Clark, John	x							x		x	x	x	9-Sr.
09 Clark, John, Jr.										x			

Person	18·00	01	02	03	04	05	06	07	08	09	10	11	Notes
11 Clark, Jonathan												x	
06 Clark, Samuel							x						
Clark, Solomon	x												
04 Clarke, William				x	x					x	x	x	
08 Clay, Thomas									x			x	
07 Clay, William								x		x	x	x	11-Sr.
11 Clay, William												x	
Clemmons, John	x		x	x	x	x	x						3-Cleamans
08 Clory, William									x				
Clup													see Culp
10 Cochran, Margaret										x			
Collier, A. Coleman	x	x		x		x				x			3-reversed
02 Collier, Clairburn			x	x		x				x	x	x	3- reversed
03 Collier, Franklin			x	x	x	x				x		x	
Collier, Hamlet	x				x	x				x	x	x	
Collier, John	x	x	x	x	x	x	x				x	x	
02 Collins, Edmund			x	x	x	x	x				x	x	
09 Collins, Eunincy										x			
03 Collins, James			x	x									
01 Collins, John		x	x										
09 Collings, Stephen										x	x	x	
03 Combs, Joseph			x	x									
11 Coney, Samuel												x	
Conway, John	x	x		x	x	x	x			x	x		
09 Coobia, Thomas										x			
02 Cook, George			x	x									
06 Cook, Jacob							x						
05 Cook, John					x			x		x			
08 Cook, John (8a)									x				
10 Cook, Peter											x	x	
10 Cooper, John											x	x	
02 Corbin, Abraham			x	x	x	x	x		x		x	x	
09 Corbin, Nathan										x			
07 Corbin, Thomas								x					
10 Cord, Ashary											x		
09 Cord, (Bethiah)										x			
07 Cord, John								x					
07 Cord, Michael								x					
07 Cord, Richard								x		x			
Corwine, George	x												
09 Cosby, Fowler										x			

Person	18	00	01	02	03	04	05	06	07	08	09	10	11	
07 Cosby, Overton									x			x	x	
Coulter, David				x	x	x	x							0/1 Cotter
11 Courtney, Elsey													x	
Cottrel, Thomas		x		x	x	x		x		x	x	x	x	
11 Cowan, Hugh													x	
Cowan, Issac		x	x	x	x	x	x	x		x	x	x	x	2-Cowin 9-Cororn
Cowan, John		x	x	x	x	x	x						x	
09 Cowan, Samuel											x			
03 Cox, John				x										
Coyle, John		x	x											
Crab, Bazel		x	x	x	x	x	x							
Craig, James		x	x	x		x		x		x				
Craig, John		x	x		x	x		x						
Craig, Margaret		x		x		x	x	x						
11 Crawford, Alexander													x	
01 Crawford, John			x	x		x	x							
06 Crawford, Mary								x	x		x		x	
Crawford, Samuel		x	x	x	x	x	x		x		x	x	x	
08 Crawford, William										x	x	x		
06 Cresswell, Potter								x	x					
09 Crips, William T.											x			
11 Crowehir, William												x		see Towhair
07 Culp, James									x			x		7-Clup
09 Culp, Thomas											x	x		9-Clup
08 Cunningham, James										x				
03 Cunningham, William				x										
08 Cuzey, James											x			

Person	18 00	01	02	03	04	05	06	07	08	09	10	11	
09 D's - 2 unknown													
Dailey, Bryan (t)	x	x	x	x									
11 Dailey, Leonard												x	11-(Darkey)
05 Dailey, Mary						x		x		x	x		9-Dagley
01 Dailey, John S.		x		x	x		x			x	x	x	9-Daisey
03 Dallis, Harvey				x									
08 Danhive, Henry									x				
05 Darland, Abraham						x	x		x	x	x	x	9-Darling
Darland, Isaac	x	x	x	x	x	x	x		x				2/3-Darling
Daugherty													see Dougherty
11 Davidson, Hugh											x		
Davidson, John	x	x				x	x		x	x	x	x	
10 Davidson, John Jr.											x		
Davidson, Thomas	x	x	x		x	x	x		x	x		x	
Davis, Eli	x	x	x	x	x	x							
03 Davis, Ishmeal				x		x			x				
Davis, Levi	x	x		x	x	x							
Davis, Philemon	x												
Davis, Robert	x	x	x	x	x	x		x		x	x	x	
03 Davis, Thomas				x		x				x	x	x	
10 Davis, Thomas (10a)											x		
02 Davis, William		x	x	x	x					x	x	x	
03 Davis, William (3a)			x		x						x		5-Jr.
Dawson, Henry	x		x	x	x								0-Dansson
Dayton, Garret	x	x	x	x	x	x	x		x	x	x	x	0/1-Dalton 8 Deyton
11 Dial, Abner											x		
11 Dial, Isaac											x		
Deal, Mathew	x	x	x	x			x		x	x	x	x	9-Dial
10 Deen, Abraham											x		
06 Dean, William						x							
03 Deatley, John			x										
09 Demitt, Henry										x	x	x	9-Dmitt 10Dew'
11 Demitt, Henry, Jr.											x		
09 Demitt, Jacob										x			9-Dmitt
03 Demoss, Lewis			x	x	x								
04 Denison, John				x									
08 Dickey, Alexander									x		x		
08 Dickey, Lawson									x				
06 Dingle, William						x			x	x	x	x	
Dils, Abraham	x	x	x	x	x				x		x	x	4Dilce 5Dilts 8 Dill
Dils, Isaac	x	x	x	x	x	x							2-Ditts 4-Dilce

Person	18	00	01	02	03	04	05	06	07	08	09	10	11	
05 Dilce, Isaac (5a)							x							
09 Dinsmore, James											x	x		
Dinsmore, Henry		x	x	x	x	x	x	x		x	x	x	x	0/1-Dinsmer
11 Dinsmore, Henry, Jr.													x	
Dinsmore, John		x		x	x		x	x		x	x		x	0/1-Dinsmer
Dinsmore, Samuel		x	x	x	x	x	x	x						0/1-Dinsmer
11 Dolly, Thomas													x	
06 Dorough, James								x			x	x		10 Dorrow
10 Dotson, Dennis											x			
08 Dotson, James										x	x	x	x	9-Datson
10 Doson, William											x			
04 Daugherty, Alex.						x								
10 Dougherty, James											x	x		
07 Douhety, Jesse								x			x	x	x	10-Daugherty
06 Doughty, John							x			x	x	x	x	10 Dougherty
11 Dougherty, John												x		
10 Doughty, Thomas										x	x	x		
06 Doughty, William							x			x	x	x		
Downey, Arch.		x	x	x	x	x	x	x		x		x	x	2/3-Downing
09 Downey, John											x			
Drake, John		x	x		x	x								
Drummond, James		x	x	x	x	x	x	x		x		x	x	0/1-Drumins
11 Duckel, John													x	
10 Dun, Abraham											x			
11 Duncon, Archibald											x	x		
05 Duncan, Armstrong						x								
03 Duncan, James				x	x	x		x		x	x	x		
01 Dunkon, Joseph			x	x	x	x	x		x		x	x	x	2/3-Duncan
02 Duncan, William				x	x	x	x		x		x	x		
11 Dupree, Thomas													x	
Duvall, Martin		x												
09 Duzan, Elizabeth											x			
Duzan, Jacob		x	x		x	x	x		x		x	x	x	3-Druzan
09 Duzan, John											x			
03 Druzan, William				x		x		x		x	x	x		5-Duzan

Person	18 00	01	02	03	04	05	06	07	08	09	10	11	
09 E's - 1 unknown													
Earlywine, Daniel	x	x	x	x	x	x	x		x	x		x	2/3/4/5-Arelywine
Earlywine, George	x	x	x	x	x	x	x		x	x	x	x	2/3/4/5-Arelywine
08 Earlywine, Jacob									x	x	x	x	
10 Earlywine, Samuel											x		
Easley, John	x	x		x									
01 Easely, Joseph		x		x						x			3-Jossah
Easly, Francis	x	x											
Easten, Phillip	x				x	x							
09 Eaton, Isaac										x			
10 Eaton, Jacob											x	x	
03 Eaton, James				x						x			
09 Eaton, John										x			
11 Edwards, Benjmain												x	
09 Edwards, Hannah										x	x	x	10-Harriet
09 Edwards, William										x			
02 Eights, William, Jr.			x										
02 Eights, William, Sr.			x										
09 Ellerback, John										x	x	x	
Ellis, John	x	x	x	x	x	x		x		x	x	x	
Ellis, James	x	x	x	x	x	x	x		x	x	x	x	6-Sr.
06 Ellis, James, Jr.							x		x		x	x	
09 Ellis, William										x		x	
Endicott													see Indicott
Enlow, Jesse	x	x	x	x	x	x	x		x	x	x	x	2/3/6/10-Inlow
02 Eslick, Francis			x		x	x	x						4-Eslake
02 Eslick, John			x										
08 Eslick, Joseph									x			x	11-Earlick
06 Eslick, Samuel							x						
02 Estes, John			x	x	x	x							
02 Estes, Thomas			x	x	x	x		x		x	x	x	10/11-Eastes
Eubanks, James	x	x					x						6-Hubanks
02 Evans, John			x	x	x	x		x	x			x	8-Evins
03 Evans, John (3a)				x		x							
03 Evins, Frances				x	x								
04 Evins, Frances (4a)					x								
10 Eavins, Rachel											x		
Eavans, Walter	x	x											

Person	18 00	01	02	03	04	05	06	07	08	09	10	11	
09 F's - 3 unknown													
Fanbs, James	x												
10 Farmer, Charles											x		
08 Farrel, James									x				
03 Faulkner, George			x		x								
Fearman, John	x	x		x	x	x		x			x	x	
02 Feeback, Frederick			x	x	x	x				x	x		
11 Feeback, John												x	
08 Ferguson, James									x				
Ferren, Hugh	x		x		x	x	x		x		x		(McFerren) 10 Fern
08 Ferren, James									x				
09 Fielder, George										x	x	x	
Fields, Benjamin	x	x			x		x						
Fields, (no name)	x												
01 Fields, Ebenzer		x	x	x	x	x		x		x	x	x	11-Fellies
01 Fields, James		x											
01 Fields, Thomas		x											
05, Fields, William						x		x		x	x	x	11-Feelas
09 (Fim), James										x			
01 Fisher, Alexander		x											
Fite, Gilbert	x												
02 Fight, Jacob			x	x	x	x	x		x	x	x	x	
Fite, John	x	x	x		x	x							2-Fight
05 Fight, Reuben						x							
04 Fight, Robert					x								
09 Fitzpatrick, James										x	x	x	
Foreman, John	x	x		x	x	x							
Forkner, George	x												
Forsyth, John	x	x	x	x	x	x	x		x		x	x	
Forsyth, Jenny(Jean)	x	x	x										
07 Foster, Aaron								x					
07 Foster, Harrison								x		x	x		
06 Foster, Jeremiah						x							
10 Foster, Rhode										x			
01 Foster, Robert		x											
Foster, Thomas	x	x		x	x	x	x		x	x			
02 Fowler, James			x			x				x	x	x	
Fowler, Luke	x	x	x	x		x			x	x	x	x	(listed in T's)
Frakes, Benjamin	x												
Frazer, James	x	x	x		x	x	x		x		x		5-Frazier
Frazer, George	x		x	x									

Person	18	00	01	02	03	04	05	06	07	08	09	10	11	
Frazer, William		x	x	x	x	x	x		x			x		5-Sr.
01 Frazer, Wm. Jr.			x		x									
10 Fry, John													x	x	
Fryer, Robert		x					x							
04 Fryer, Thomas						x								
01 Fryman, George			x	x		x	x	x		x	x		x	4-Friman
10 Fryman, Henry												x	x	
Fryman, Phillip		x	x	x		x	x		x		x	x	x	
05 Fryman, Philip, Jr.							x		x		x			
01 Fryman, Robert			x											
11 Fuller, Harrich													x	
06 Fuller, Joseph								x		x	x	x	x	
09 Fulton, John											x		x	
03 Fulton, Samuel					x		x	x			x	x	x	

Person	18 00	01	02	03	04	05	06	07	08	09	10	11	
09 G's - 4 unknown													
05 Gabriel, Thomas					x					x			9-Gambriel
10 Gadman, William											x		
Gamble, David	x	x	x	x	x	x	x	x		x		x	
04 Gaffen, Oath					x	x	x					x	
Galbreath, Andrew	x												
Galbreath, Benjamin	x	x	x	x	x	x	x		x	x	x	x	2-Jalbreath 8 Bal'
09 Galbreath, Benjamin, Jr.										x			
11 Galbreath, Daniel												x	
Galbreath, John	x	x	x	x	x	x							2-Jalbreath
Galbreath, William	x	x	x	x	x	x	x		x	x	x		2-Jalbreath
01 Garnet, Philip K.		x											
Gateral, Thomas ('rell)	x	x	x	x		x		x		x			0-Gattinel 3-Gatingel
Geoghegan, John	x	x	x	x	x	x	x			x	x	x	0-Goehegan
08 Geoghegan, John, Jr.									x	x	x	x	
02 Geoghegan, Michael			x	x	x	x	x				x		
07 (George), John								x					
02 Gibson, Thomas			x	x		x		x					
04 Gillaspie, James					x		x			x	x	x	6-Gallaspe
Githens, Henry	x	x	x	x	x	x	x		x	x	x	x	0/1Gidions 2Geathens
Githens, James	x	x		x	x	x	x		x	x	x		0/1Gidions 9Gwaithin
Githens, John	x	x	x	x	x	x			x		x	x	0/1Gidions 2 Gthens
09 Gwaithins, Thomas										x			
10 Glasscock, Cena											x		
Glasscock, Daniel	x	x	x										
Glasscock, Daniel(0a)	x	x											
02 Glascock, Jesse			x										
10 Glasscock, Peggy											x		
Glasscock, Samuel	x	x	x										
Glassgow, James	x	x		x								x	
09 Glen, Elijah										x			
09 Glen, Simone										x	x		
10 Godsey, Gilbert											x		
Gonce, George	x	x	x		x	x	x		x	x	x	x	2-Gones
Gonce, Nicholas	x	x			x	x	x		x	x	x	x	6-Gaunce
02 Gonsollus, James			x	x	x	x				x	x		3-Gunsaullus
10 Gonsallas, Thomas											x	x	
08 Gorman, Daniel									x	x	x	x	
Gowsnel, William	x	x											1-Gonslen
09-Gragg, Joseph										x	x	x	
02 Graham, James			x	x	x	x	x		x		x	x	

Person	18	00	01	02	03	04	05	06	07	08	09	10	11	
03 Grant, Jonathan					x									
Gray, Anny		x	x	x										
Gray, David		x	x	x	x	x	x		x	x	x	x	x	2-Grey
Gray, David (0a)		x	x		x	x	x				x	x	x	11-Jr.
01 Gray, James			x	x	x	x	x	x				x	x	
02 Gray, James (2a)				x	x									
03 Gray, James					x									
03 Gray, John					x									
03 Gray, John					x	x								
Gray, Joseph		x	x	x	x									
09 Gray, Isaac											x	x	x	11-Sr.
11 Gray, Isaac, Jr.													x	
01 Gray, Robert			x											
02 Gray, William				x						x	x			
09 Green, David											x			
11 Green, William													x	
09 Green, Zachariah											x	x		
Griffin, Gabriel		x	x		x	x	x		x			x	x	
01 Griffith, Joseph			x											
05 Griffith, Martin							x			x	x	x	x	
11 Griffith, Samuel													x	
Grosvener, Richard		x	x		x	x	x		x		x	x	x	0'Grossowmer3 'vines
Guften, Amos		x												
11 Gulley, William													x	

Person	18	00	01	02	03	04	05	06	07	08	09	10	11	
09 H's - 2 unknown														
03 Hadden, Thomas					x		x	x		x				
06 Hains, George								x	x			x	x	10/11-Hanes
Hall, Benjamin		x	x	x	x	x	x	x			x	x	x	x	
Hall, Cornelius		x	x	x	x	x	x	x			x	x	x	x	
03 Hall, Cornelius, Jr.						x	x	x							
09 Hall, Elihu												x		x	
Hall, James		x	x	x	x		x				x	x	x	x	
11 Hall, John														x	
Hall, Moses		x	x	x	x	x	x	x			x	x	x	x	
02 Hall, Robert					x	x	x	x	x		x	x	x	x	
09 Hall, Samuel												x	x	x	
Hall, Thomas		x	x	x	x										
02 Hall, William					x	x	x	x	x		x	x	x	x	
03 Hallman, John						x									
Hamilton, Abd.		x	x	x											
03 Hammelton, Alexander						x	x	x	x						
09 Hamilton, Daniel												x			
Hamilton, Elias		x	x					x							
02 Hamilton, James				x	x	x	x	x	x	x				x	2-Hammelton
Hamilton, James, Jr.		x	x	x				x							2-Hammelton
Hamilton, John		x	x	x	x	x	x	x			x	x	x	x	2-Hammelton
Hamilton, Robert		x						x							
Hamilton, Samuel		x	x												
02 Hamilton, Thomas				x			x					x			2- Hammelton
04 Hamilton, William							x	x							
04 Handley, Thomas							x								
Hanna, Samuel		x	x	x	x										2/3-Hannah
Harden, Elihu		x	x	x	x	x	x			x		x	x	x	
01 Harden, James			x	x	x	x	x			x					
02 Harden, John					x	x	x			x		x	x		9-Hardik
11 Harden, Thomas													x		
11 Harden, William													x		
11 Hardy, Armstead													x		
01 Harlen, Moses			x	x	x	x	x								
Harmen, Robert	x	x													
Harmesson, Wallace	x														
Harney, Hiram		x	x	x	x	x	x			x		x	x	x	
Harney, Mills		x	x	x	x	x	x			x		x	x	x	
Harney, Rollen		x	x	x	x	x	x			x		x	x	x	
02 Harney, Thomas				x	x	x	x			x		x	x	x	

Person	1800	01	02	03	04	05	06	07	08	09	10	11	
03 Harrison, Anne				x									
03 Harrison, Benjamin				x									
02 Harrison, Lawrence			x	x	x	x							
Hariston, John	x												
06 Harson, George							x						
Harson, Garrett	x	x		x	x	x							0/1-Harison, Garrard
Hart, Zepheniah	x												
10 Hartley, Elizabeth											x		
08 Hartley, John									x				
08 Hartley, Mordicai									x	x		x	
05 Hartley, Thomas						x	x						6-Harley
03 Hartsock, Isaac				x	x	x							3-Harback
10 Hartsock, Samuel											x		
06 Haslet, Samuel							x			x	x	x	
09 Hazlett, William										x			
08 Hawkins, Gregory									x	x			
Hawkins, Samuel	x	x	x		x	x			x	x	x	x	
02 Hawkins, Samuel (2a)			x		x			x					
Hawkins, Thomas	x	x	x	x		x	x		x	x	x	x	
11 Hayse, Gabriel												x	
02 Heavens, William			x										
Helpman, John	x	x	x		x	x			x	x			9-Helpenson
11 Henderson, William												x	
04 Hendrix, John					x				x	x			9-Henico10
10 Henry, John											x	x	
08 Herbert, William									x		x	x	10/11-Harbert
07 Hiatt, Shadrack								x			x	x	10/11-Hyatt
Hildreth, Squire	x	x		x	x	x		x		x	x	x	1-Hildridge
09 Hildreth, William										x			
Hill, James	x	x	x	x	x	x	x		x	x	x	x	
Hill, John	x	x	x	x	x	x	x		x	x	x		
06 Hill, Richard							x			x		x	
10 Hillick, (Alvin)											x		
11 Hillock, Edward												x	
11 Hillock, James												x	
03 Hines, George				x									
03 Hines, Jacob				x	x	x							
02 Hinton, Ezekiel			x	x		x	x		x	x	x	x	
09 Hisas, Daniel										x			
02 Hisler, John			x	x									
01 Hisler, William		x											

Person	18	00	01	02	03	04	05	06	07	08	09	10	11	
07 Hitch, Wise									x			x		see Wiseman
Hixson, Benjamin		x												
Hizer, Jacob														see Hyson
Holladay, William (i)		x	x	x		x	x	x			x		x	x	8 Holy'
10 Holler, Francis													x		
07 Hollar, John									x		x		x	9-Holler
11 Hollman, John														x	
03 Holly, Thompson					x	x	x		x		x	x	x	4-Tom Hollow
09 Holmes, Jackson											x			
03 Honical, Jacob					x	x	x		x		x	x	x	4-Honcan
02 Hopkins, David				x										
09 Hopkins, Elihu											x	x		
10 (Hosen, Moshan)												x		
11 How, Amos													x	
08 How, Ezra										x			x	
02 How, Samuel				x	x	x	x	x		x	x	x	x	5-Howe
11 Howard, Eli													x	
03 Howard, Ephraim					x	x				x				
Howard, Gidion		x				x	x			x	x	x	x	
10 Howard, Gidion (10a)												x	x	
06 Howard, Henry								x		x	x	x	x	
01 Howard, Jacob			x			x	x			x	x	x	x	
Howard, Mary		x	x											
09 Howard, Mathew											x			
04 Howard, Vachel						x	x							
02 Howard, William				x	x	x	x							
09 Howerton, George											x	x	x	
03 Huddleston, Allexander					x	x	x	x		x		x	x	5-Heddleston
03 Huddleston, John					x	x								
08 Hudson, Major										x		x		
10 Huffman, Abe												x		
Huffman, Peter		x	x	x	x	x	x	x		x	x		x	0/1-Hofman
02 Hughes, James				x										
05 Hughes, Robert							x							
02 Hughs, (Taubler)					x	x			x					8-Tolvert
09 Hudges, Solomon											x			
Hughes, William		x	x		x	x	x			x	x	x	x	0/1-Hugh
11 Hughes, William, Jr.													x	
11 Hunter, James													x	
Hunter, John		x	x	x		x	x		x			x	x	
04 Hustens, Henry						x								

Person	18	00	01	02	03	04	05	06	07	08	09	10	11	
01 Huston, John			x	x	x	x									0/1-Housten
02 Huston, John (2a)				x											
Hyson, Jacob (*)		x	x		x										1-Hizer

Person	18	00	01	02	03	04	05	06	07	08	09	10	11	
11 Indicott, Jacob														x	
03 Indicott, Joseph					x	x	x			x					3-Indient 7-Endi'
07 Indicott, Thomas										x					
07 Ungles, John										x		x	x	x	listed in U's
07 Ingles, Peter										x		x	x		
06 Irvin, Andrew									x		x	x	x	x	
06 Irvin, Caleb									x			x			
Irvin, David		x	x												
10 Irvin, George													x	x	
08 Irvin, John											x				
09 Irvin, Joshua												x			
05 Irvin, Samuel							x					x		x	
01 Ishmal, Benjamin			x	x	x	x	x	x							2-Eshmale
04 Ishmail, James					x	x	x					x		x	
10 Ishmail, John													x	x	
08 Ishmail, Thomas										x			x	x	

90

Person	18	00	01	02	03	04	05	06	07	08	09	10	11	Notes
11 Jackson, John													x	
08 Jacoby, Daniel										x				
02 x Janbe x, George				x							x			9-Javis
10 (Javinall), David												x	x	11-Juvinall
Jenins, Solomon		x		x		x	x				x			6-Jinsons 9Jennings
10 Jenkins, Mary											x			
Jinkins, Samuel		x	x	x	x	x	x							
09 Jenkins, Thomas											x		x	
07 Jinkins, William									x		x			
03 Johnson, Allexander					x									
01 Johnston, Arthur			x											
01 Johnston, Isom					x	x	x	x			x	x	x	
Johnston, James		x		x	x	x			x		x	x	x	9-Johnson
Johnston, James (0a)		x									x	x	x	
02 Johnston, (Jason)				x										
05 Johnston, Jean						x								
04 Johnson, John						x	x				x	x		
Johnston, John Jr.		x	x	x	x	x		x		x				
Johnston, John Sr.		x	x	x	x	x	x	x		x	x		x	
10 Johnson, Joseph											x	x		
Johnston, Jonathan		x	x	x	x			x			x			
Johnston, Lewis		x	x											
Johnston, Major		x	x								x			
02 Johnston, Mason				x	x	x	x		x			x	x	11-Marion
02 Johnston, William				x	x	x	x	x		x	x	x		
11 Jolly, Daniel												x		
Jolly, David		x	x	x	x	x	x	x		x	x	x		3-Golly
08 Jones, Daniel										x				
08 Jones, Drury										x	x	x	x	
03 Jones, George				x	x	x			x					
02 Jones, Israel			x		x									
Jones, Jacob		x	x	x	x	x	x	x	x	x	x	x	x	5-Sr.
Jones, Jacob (0a)		x	x	x	x	x	x	x		x	x		x	5-Jr.
Jones, Jacob (0b)		x				x								
Jones, John		x	x	x	x	x	x	x		x	x	x		
Jones, John, Jr.		x	x	x	x	x	x	x		x	x			
04 Jones, John (4a)						x								
02 Jones, Major			x	x										
03 Jones, Mays				x										
Jones, Moses		x	x			x	x				x	x	x	
02 Jones, Nicholas			x	x					x					

Person	18	00	01	02	03	04	05	06	07	08	09	10	11
07 Jones, Robert									x				
09 Jones, Samuel											x		
Jones, Thomas		x	x	x	x	x	x	x					
Jones, William		x	x	x	x	x	x		x				
Jones, William (0a)		x											
Jorden, William		x	x										

Person	18 00	01	02	03	04	05	06	07	08	09	10	11	
09 K's - 4 unknown													
04/5 Karnahan													see Carnahan
09 Kasey													see Casey
Keys, John	x	x	x	x	x	x							0/1-Kays
01 Keysey, James		x		x		x							see Casesey
07 Keath, Adam								x		x	x	x	
Keith, Jacob	x	x	x	x	x	x		x		x	x	x	7-Keath
Keith, Phillip	x	x	x	x	x	x		x		x	x	x	
04 Kelly, Thomas					x	x				x	x		
Kennedy, Andrew	x								x	x	x		
Kenedy, David	x				x		x		x	x	x		
08 Kennedy, Nathaniel									x				
06 Kennedy, Robert							x			x	x		
04 Kenney, Alexander					x	x							
02 Kenton, Elizabeth			x	x	x	x							
Kinten, Phillip	x	x		x	x	x		x					3-Kenten/on
Kentt, John	x												
05 Kerns, Adam						x	x			x	x		10 Carns
11 Kersin, Isabella												x	
07 Ketherwood													see Catherwood
03 Kiles, John				x	x	x				x		x	9-Kite
06 Kilgore, John							x						
01 Killgore, Oliver		x	x	x									
Killgore, William	x	x	x	x	x	x			x	x	x	x	5-Gilgore
08 Kimbrough, Elizabeth									x	x	x	x	
Kimbrough, John	x	x		x	x	x		x		x	x	x	0/1-Kimbro
01 Kimbrough, Nathaniel		x	x	x	x	x	x						2-Cimbrough
Kimbrough, Richard	x			x	x	x				x	x		0/1/2-Kimbro
07 Kimbrough, Robert								x		x	x	x	
Kimbrough, Samuel	x	x	x	x	x	x		x					0-Kimbro
11 Kimbrough, Susanna												x	
11 Kincade, George												x	
02 Kincart, James			x	x	x		x		x	x	x	x	
08 Kincart, John									x	x	x	x	
Kincart, Samuel	x	x		x	x	x	x		x	x	x	x	
10 King, Barnett										x			
04 Kinney, Alexander					x								
09 Krusor, Michael										x	x	x	

Person	1800	01	02	03	04	05	06	07	08	09	10	11	
06 Lamaster, Abraham							x						
05 Lambert, Barnabus						x							
Leach, Benjamin	x												
Lee, George	x												
Leeper, John	x	x	x	x	x	x	x		x	x	x	x	8-Leaper
Leeper, William	x	x	x	x	x	x	x		x	x			
Leonard, Michael	x	x	x	x	x	x							2-Lennard
Leonard, Valentine	x	x											
Lilly, Anieger	x	x	x	x	x	x	x			x			2-Armager 9Amerigo
Lilly, Pleasant	x	x	x		x			x		x	x	x	3-xx out
03 Little, Kinsey				x									
02 Livingood, George	x	x	x	x	x	x		x		x	x	x	0/1-Leavengood
Livingston, David	x	x	x	x	x	x							
09 Liuzy, David										x			
Loan, Isaac	x	x											
04 Logan, David				x	x		x			x	x	x	
09 Lockridge, James										x	x	x	
Loughridge, John	x	x	x	x	x	x	x		x	x	x	x	2-Loughrage 8Lawhr'
03 Lockridge, Robert			x	x	x							x	
Lockridge, William	x	x	x	x		x	x			x	x	x	0/1-Loughridge
Long, Benjamin	x		x										
03 Long, Eliakain			x	x	x	x							4-Lakin
03 Long, Samuel			x	x	x	x			x	x	x	x	
08 Longdon, Edmond									x				
Louderback, Andrew	x	x	x	x	x	x		x		x	x	x	9-Lauderback
05 Lowderback, Peter						x							
Low, George	x	x		x	x	x		x		x	x	x	0-Lars 9-Lowe
08 Low, Isaac									x	x	x	x	
01 Low, William		x	x	x	x	x	x						
02 Lyon, Alexander			x	x									

Person	1800	01	02	03	04	05	06	07	08	09	10	11	
09 M's - 15 unknown													
10 Maddan, Susan											x		see Mathers
10 Maffett, Henry											x	x	
07 Maffett, Matthew								x		x		x	
03 Moffet, Thomas				x	x	x		x		x	x	x	5-Mofford 7Maffett
07 Maffett, William								x		x	x	x	
04 Mahan, Thomas					x								
Man, George	x	x	x	x									
02 Man, Henry			x		x	x	x			x			
Man, Jacob	x	x	x	x	x	x	x		x	x			
Man, John	x	x	x			x	x		x	x	x	x	
01 Man, Peter		x	x	x	x	x	x		x	x		x	
10 Manin, H.											x		
10 Manin, Jacob											x		
11 Mannon, John												x	
06 Mannens, Meredith							x			x	x	x	6-'er 9 Kenneth
06 Mannens, Samuel							x		x	x	x	x	6'er 8'on 9Mansire
10 Marell-----											x		
02 Marsh, Beal			x	x									
01 Marsh, Dial		x											
Marsh, Thomas	x	x	x	x	x	x	x		x	x	x	x	
03 Marsh, William				x									
Marshall, Archibald	x	x	x	x	x	x	x		x		x	x	3-Alexander
Marshall, David	x	x	x							x	x	x	
08 Marshall, Hugh									x	x	x	x	
09 Marshall, James										x			
09 Marshall, John										x			
Marshall, Ralph	x	x		x	x	x				x			3-Realph
Marshall, Samuel	x		x	x	x	x		x		x	x		
11 Marshall, William												x	
03 Martin, James				x						x	x		
Martain, John	x	x	x	x	x	x		x		x			
Martain, John (0a)	x		x	x									
02 Martin, John (2a)		x											
02 Martin, John (2b)		x											
07 Martin, Joseph								x					
10 Martin, Michael											x		(Mastin)
02 Marten Nehemiah		x	x	x	x		x		x		x		
02 Martin, Samuel		x		x						x			
Martain, Zedehiah	x	x	x	x	x	x		x					
09 Masen, Benjamin										x		x	11-Mason

95

Person	1800	01	02	03	04	05	06	07	08	09	10	11	
Mason, Burgess	x	x	x	x	x	x		x		x		x	2-Mayson 9 Masen
08 Massett, James									x				
06 Mathers, Gian							x		x	x	x	x	8-Garvin
08 Mathers, James									x		x	x	
11 Mathers, John												x	
Mathers, Samuel	x	x			x	x	x	x		x			
Mathers, William	x	x	x	x	x	x	x		x	x	x	x	3-Madders
06 Mathers, William, Jr.							x			x			
04Mattlock /Mattox, Elijah					x	x		x		x			7/9 Mattox
Matlock, Samuel	x	x		x	x	x							3-Metlock
11 Maxwell, Gavin												x	
06 Maxwell, William						x		x	x			x	
11 Maynard, Jeremiah												x	
10 Maynor, Jesse											x		
02 McCabe, Jossiah			x	x	x	x		x		x	x	x	
01 McCall, James		x	x	x	x	x			x	x	x	x	
02 McCall, James (2a)			x	x									
09 McCall, John										x	x	x	
04 McCall, R. James					x								
10 McChan, Daniel											x		
02 McCan, James			x	x									
09 McCan, William										x			
03 McCarnahan, Robert				x									
McCarty, David	x	x	x	x	x	x		x		x	x	x	
McCarty, David, Jr.	x												
11 McCarty, Felix												x	
01 McCarty, Thomas		x	x	x	x	x		x		x	x	x	
09 McClain, Charles										x	x		10-McCain
McClannahan, James	x	x	x	x	x	x	x		x		x	x	2-McClanagen
09 McClingan, Joseph										x			
McClannahan, Wm.	x			x	x	x	x		x	x	x	x	9-McClinagin
McClintock, Hugh	x	x	x	x	x	x	x		x	x	x	x	
McClintock, Joseph	x	x	x	x	x	x	x	x	x		x	x	2- McK 6-Clintock
McClintock, Joseph, Jr.	x	x	x	x	x	x				x			
11 McClintock, Thomas												x	
11 McClintock, William												x	
McClurgh, Joseph	x	x	x	x	x	x				x	x	x	
01 (McComs/Guin), Jas.		x											
10 McConice, Christopher											x		
09 McConahan, Achilles										x			
McCord, David	x	x	x	x	x	x		x		x	x	x	see Cord

Person	18	00	01	02	03	04	05	06	07	08	09	10	11	
03 McCord, John					x				x		x	x	x	
McCord, Michael		x	x	x	x	x	x		x		x	x	x	
McCord, William		x	x	x	x	x	x		x		x	x		
McCord, William, Sr.		x	x	x	x								x	
07 McCormick, Adam									x				x	
05 McCormick, Elizabeth							x	x		x	x	x	x	11-Widdow
McCormach, James		x	x	x	x	x							x	
McCormick, James		x	x	x										
McCormick, John		x												
02 McCormick, Samuel				x	x									
McCotten, John		x												
01 McCouns, Lawrenis			x									x		10-McCown, 'rence
11 McCoy, Andrew													x	
06 McCoy, Daniel							x			x		x		
11 McCoy, David													x	
McCracken, John		x	x											
McCracken, John (0a)		x	x											
11 McCune, Gavin													x	
09 McCune, James											x			
McCune, John		x	x	x	x	x	x	x		x	x	x	x	5-Sr.
McCune, Robert		x	x	x	x	x	x	x		x	x	x	x	
05 McCune, Robert, Jr.						x	x			x	x	x	x	
03 McCuthen, Thomas					x	x	x							
03 McDaniel, William					x			x	x					
10 McDole, James											x			
10 McDole, William											x			
McDonal, Alexander		x	x	x	x	x	x	x	x	x	x	x	x	2-McDannal 6-Sr.
McDonald, Alexander		x		x		x	x	x			x	x		9-McDanald
McDonald, George		x	x	x	x		x	x		x	x	x	x	2-McDannal
09 McDanold, John										x	x			
McDonald, Joseph		x				x	x	x		x	x	x	x	
10 McDanald, Mary											x			
McDonald, Mordicay		x	x		x	x	x	x		x		x	x	
McDonald, William		x	x	x	x		x				x			2-McDannal 9'Donnel
05 McDoogle, William							x							
04 McDowell, Burgess					x									
04 McDowell, James					x		x		x			x		
04 McDowell, John					x		x							
01 McDowell, Mary			x		x		x				x			(10 no surname)
11 McDowel, Margaret												x		
McDowell, William		x	x			x		x		x	x			

97

Person	18 00	01	02	03	04	05	06	07	08	09	10	11	
03 McFall, Whittington				x									
05 McFarland, John					x								
McFarland, William	x	x	x	x	x	x		x		x	x	x	2-McFarling
03 McFarland, William(3a)				x									
03 McFarris, Hugh				x									
McPherren, James	x												
McFerren, Samuel	x		x		x		x		x				4-McPh
McFerren, William	x	x	x		x								(see Ferren)
01 McGinnis, William		x	x	x	x	x	x		x	x	x		
10 McGlolan, John										x			
10 McGlolan, John (10a)										x			(looks duplicated)
03 McGriff, John				x									
McGriff, Richard	x	x	x	x	x	x							
10 McGuire, John										x	x		
McIntire, Andrew	x												
08 McIntire, Joseph								x	x	x			
McIntire, Robert	x	x	x	x	x	x	x						
03 McKee, Hugh				x									
McKee, James	x			x									
07 Mcmckeen, Archible							x						
01 McKinley, George		x	x	x									
09 McLaughlin, John										x		x	
11 McLaughlin, John (11a)												x	
11 McLaughlin, William												x	
11 McLean, Charles												x	
03 McLease, William			x	x	x	x		x		x	x		4'Cleebe,5'Clees,8'Lees
11 McMahan, John												x	
McMahan, Robert	x	x	x		x	x	x		x	x	x	x	
10 McMahan, Robert (10a)										x			
11 McMehan, Archibald												x	
04 McMihell, John				x	x	x						x	5-McMichell
06 McMichel, Thomas						x			x	x	x		9McMihil
08 McMickle, William								x					
09 McNulty, James									x	x	x		11-McAnally
09 McNulty, John									x		x		
McNulty, Joseph	x	x	x	x	x	x	x		x	x	x	x	2McInutty 6McAnulty
McPherren, James	x												see McFerren
06 McRight, Matthew						x							
11 McShain, Daniel												x	
McShan, Sarah	x	x											1-McShain
09 McQuion, Lawrence									x		x		

Person	18	00	01	02	03	04	05	06	07	08	09	10	11	
09 Mear, Samuel											x			
Megines, William		x												
10 Menach, Alexander												x	x	
06 Meenach, William								x						
Menteen, John		x												
Menteen, Robert		x	x											
10 Meredith, Absolum												x		
09 Merit, Thomas											x			
Metcalf, Eli		x	x	x	x	x	x		x		x	x	x	
Metcalf, Rhodey		x												
Metcalf, Thomas		x	x	x	x	x	x		x			x	x	2-Matcalf
Miller, Abraham		x	x		x				x		x		x	
07 Miller, Abraham, Jr.									x		x		x	
09 Miller, James											x	x	x	
01 Miller, John			x											
Miller, William		x	x	x	x	x	x							
10 Mitchel, Ezekiel												x	x	
Mitchel, James		x	x	x	x	x								
Mitchel, John		x	x	x					x					
11 Mitchel, Joseph													x	
Mitchel, Robert		x		x										
05 Mitchel, (Queen)							x							
Mitchel, William		x	x											
11 Mitcheltree, John													x	
Mitcheltree, Josias		x	x	x	x	x	x				x			3-Mitchel
01 Mitcheltree, Thomas			x	x	x	x								
Moffett														see Maffett
07 Molden, William									x					
08 Moler, Isaac									x	x	x			
03 Monday, Harrison				x										
Mollholand, Patrick		x	x	x	x	x								0/1-Monhollen
09 Monicle, Christopher											x	x	x	
04 Monigal, George					x	x					x	x		
02 Monical, Peter			x		x	x				x	x	x		4-Monigal
01 Montcrief, Elizabeth			x	x	x	x								2-Vancriff
07 Moncreath, Wilson										x				
02 Montear, John			x											
02 Montear, Robert			x	x										
03 Montgomery, James				x	x									
02 Moore, John			x	x			x		x		x			
03 Moor, John				x		x								

99

Person	18 00	01	02	03	04	05	06	07	08	09	10	11	
Moore, Samuel	x	x	x	x		x	x		x		x	x	
11 Moore, Samuel, Jr.												x	
04 Moor, William				x									
08 Morgan, Agnes									x		x	x	
Morgan, Charles	x	x	x	x	x	x				x	x	x	
Morgan, David	x	x	x	x					x				
02 Morgan, David (2a)			x										
Morgan, Garret	x	x	x	x	x	x	x		x	x	x	x	2/3-Garrard 8Jared
06 Morgan, George							x						
01 Morgan, James		x			x								
Morgan, John	x	x	x	x	x	x	x						
Morgan, Joseph	x	x	x	x	x	x						x	
Morgan, Rece	x												
Morris, Jacob	x	x	x	x	x								
11 Morris, John												x	
10 Morris, Morris											x	x	
Morris, Thomas	x	x	x	x	x	x	x				x	x	
(Morton, Throck), John*	x												Throckmorton
10 Mullin, Samuel										x	x		
10 Munson, Joel											x	x	11-Monson
02 Murdock, McDannal			x										
Murphey, W. George	x	x	x	x	x	x	x			x	x	x	
05 Murphy, Zepheniah						x	x		x	x	x	x	
11 Myers, Abraham												x	
05 Myers, Alexander						x							
11 Myers, Christian												x	
11 Myers, Daniel												x	
02 Myers, David	x						x		x	x	x	x	
Myers, George	x	x	x	x	x	x	x		x	x		x	6-Miers
11 Myers, Henry												x	
04 Myers, Jacob				x	x								4-Myans
Myers, John	x	x	x	x	x	x	x		x	x	x	x	
06 Miers, Lewis							x		x			x	8-Myers
08 Myers, Margaret									x	x	x	x	

Person	18	00	01	02	03	04	05	06	07	08	09	10	11	
10 Neaves, Daniel												x	x	
11 Neaves, Walter													x	
08 Nelson, Moses										x		x	x	
10 Nesbet, John												x		
Nesbet, Nathan		x	x	x	x	x	x	x					x	6-Nathaniel
01 Nesbet, Samuel			x	x	x									
Nesbet, Thomas		x	x	x		x	x	x		x		x	x	
10 Nesbet, Thomas (10a)												x		
Nicholas, John		x												
Nickel, Robert		x	x	x	x	x	x	x		x		x	x	2-Nicholas
Newcum, Daniel		x	x	x	x							x		1-Nucum 3-Nukim
09 Nudigate, John											x	x	x	
Nudigate, William		x	x	x	x	x	x		x		x	x	x	
10 N-------, Yancy												x		

Person	18	00	01	02	03	04	05	06	07	08	09	10	11	
10 Obadiah,---												x		
03 O'Cansan, William					x									
Oden, William		x	x	x	x	x	x							
10 Ogdon, Mary												x		
11 Olfrey, James													x	
10 Olanan, Susan												x		
03 Olliver, Elizabeth					x	x	x	x		x				
Oliver, John		x	x	x	x	x	x		x			x	x	
10 Olliver, Thomas												x		
03 Oliver, Widow					x									
10 Orr, John												x		
10 Overby, Henry												x	x	
07 Overfield, Moses									x			x	x	
04 Overfield, Paul						x	x							

Person	18	00	01	02	03	04	05	06	07	08	09	10	11	
09 P's 1 unknown														
09 Padget, Daniel											x	x	x	
08 Packstone, Robert										x				
03 Paine, Daniel					x									
Palmer, Robert		x	x			x								4-Pamlor
05 Paneton, John							x							
Parks, James		x	x	x	x					x		x	x	
01 Parks, Joseph			x					x						
Parks, Robert		x	x	x		x	x	x						
03 Parson, John					x	x	x	x				x	x	3-Person
10 Parter, James												x		
06 Patchel, John								x						(Panhel)
08 Patton, Robert, Jr.										x				
09 Patton, Robert, Sr.											x			
02 Patton, Stephen				x								x		
04 Pough, Benjamin						x	x							
Paugh, Henry		x	x											1-Pough
03 Paugh, Sarah					x	x	x	x		x				
11 Pauley, Abraham													x	
06 Pauley, Isaac								x		x				
04 Pauley, John						x	x	x		x	x	x	x	9 Pawley
08 Pauley, John, Jr.										x				
04 Pauley, William						x	x	x		x			x	
Paxton, Robert		x	x	x			x	x				x	x	
Payton														see Peyton
01 Pendergrass, Edward			x	x	x	x	x	x		x		x	x	
10 Pecherer, Nancy												x		
04 Peers, Valentine						x	x							5-Pairs (see Airs ?)
Perren, C. William		x	x											
03 Payton, Robert					x									
Peyton, Samuel		x	x	x	x	x		x		x		x	x	
Peyton, Stephen		x	x		x	x	x	x		x		x	x	
06 Peyton, Stephen, Jr.								x		x		x	x	
Peyton, Thomas		x	x	x	x	x	x	x		x		x	x	2-
Payton														
Peyton, William		x	x	x	x	x	x							
07 Pheber, Frederick									x					
10 Phillip, John												x	x	10-(Donan)
10 Phillips, Joshua												x		
Phillip, Michal		x												
08 Plew, Daniel										x	x			9-Pleugh

102

Person	18 00	01	02	03	04	05	06	07	08	09	10	11	
Plew, Elias	x	x	x	x	x	x	x		x	x	x		1-Plue 3-Plough
Plew, Jeremiah	x	x	x	x	x	x	x		x	x	x	x	1-Plue 3 Plough
Plew, Philip	x					x						x	
03 Poe, Benjamin				x			x						
03 Poe, William				x	x		x			x		x	
Polley, John	x	x	x	x									
01 Potts, Frederick		x					x				x		
10 Pots, Samuel										x			
Potts, William	x	x	x	x	x				x	x	x	x	
Porter, John	x	x											
Porter, Thomas	x	x											
Porter, William	x								x				
01 Powel, Charles		x	x	x	x	x	x		x		x	x	
04 Powel, George				x	x		x			x			
08 Powel, Isaac									x			x	
05 Powel, Jeremiah					x	x			x		x	x	
10 Powel, Jerry											x		11-Power
04 Powel, John					x	x	x		x	x	x	x	
02 Powel, Milley			x										
05 Powel, Samuel						x							
Powel, Thomas	x	x	x	x	x	x	x		x	x	x	x	
05 Powel, Thomas, Jr.						x			x		x	x	
10 Powel, William											x		10-Power
04 Powel, Zenis					x	x	x		x		x	x	
10 Prather, Ashford											x	x	
09 Prather, Benjamin										x			
05 Prater, Jeremiah						x		x			x	x	7-Sr.
07 Prater, Jeremiah, Jr.								x			x	x	
04 Price, Christopher					x	x							
Price, John	x			x	x	x							
05 Price, John, Jr.						x							
Pritchet, William	x	x	x	x	x	x		x			x	x	1-Protchet 5-Pritchell
11 Porvel, George												x	(Powel ?)
05 Pullen, James						x							
Pumel, Every	x												
Pumel, William	x	x											
03 Pursley, Thomas				x	x	x					x	x	10-Purcell
02 Pursley, William	x		x	x		x	x				x	x	2-Purnal 5-Purnell
09 Qualer, John										x			

Person	1800	01	02	03	04	05	06	07	08	09	10	11	
Rachford, Robert	x												
01 Ragsdale, Drury		x				x		x					8-Drusa
09 Rafter, Asain										x			
09 Ramsey, Archibald										x	x	x	
08(Randall), Richard									x	x		x	9-Rannals
02 Rankin, Moses			x	x	x	x		x		x		x	
03 Rawlings, Samuel				x									
Razor, Henry	x	x	x										
Ray, Francis, Sr.	x	x	x	x	x		x	x	x	x	x	x	4-Sr.
05 Ray, Francis, Jr.				x	x								
Ray, James	x	x	x	x			x		x	x			
Ray, Samuel	x		x	x	x								
02 Reding, Eli		x									x	x	
03 Redding, William			x	x	x	x		x	x		x	x	4-Reading
01 Reed, Isaac		x	x	x									
Reed, William	x	x	x			x							
10 Retzel, Peter											x	x	11-Retzatt
06 Reveal, James						x		x					
Reveal, Joseph	x	x	x	x	x	x	x		x	x	x	x	0/1-Reviel 10 Riveel
06 Reveal, Michael							x			x	x	x	
Reveal, Thomas	x			x	x	x	x		x	x	x	x	0/1-Reviel
Rhodes													see Roads
11 Rice, Jany												x	
02 Richards, Isaac			x										
05 Richard, William						x			x			x	5-Richarts
02 Rily, Iosah			x										
Reily, John	x	x	x	x	x	x	x		x		x	x	2-Rily 3-Ryley
03 Riley, Robert				x									
07 Ritche, Asy								x		x	x	x	9 Asaph 11Esau
Richey, Gilbert	x							x			x	x	
Richey, Isaac	x			x	x	x		x		x	x	x	7-Ritche
09 Ritchy, Noah										x	x	x	
Richey, Robert	x	x	x		x	x	x		x	x	x	x	
02 Richey, Robert (2a)			x										
06 Richee, Solomon							x				x	x	
06 Richee, William							x				x		
Riddel, William	x	x			x	x	x						see Ruddle
Roase, Abraham	x												(Robeson ?)
Roads, Becham	x	x	x	x	x	x	x		x		x	x	0/1-Rhoads
11 Robb, William												x	
09 Rhodes, Benjamin										x			

Person	18	00	01	02	03	04	05	06	07	08	09	10	11	
09 Rhodes, Silas											x	x	x	11-Roads
03 Roberts. Abigail					x	x	x							5-Argile
04 Roberts, Azariah						x	x	x		x				
06 Roberts, Ezekiel								x						
10 Roberts, John												x	x	
Roberts, Henly	x	x	x	x	x	x	x			x	x	x	x	2-Hely 3-Hanley
01 Roberts, Hezekiah			x	x	x	x	x			x	x	x		
02 Roberts, Manly				x										
02 Roberts, Miner				x										
02 Roberts, Nehamiah				x								x		
01 Roberts, Neily			x		x	x	x				x			
06 Roberts, Sarah								x						
Roberts, Thomas	x		x	x	x	x	x			x	x	x	x	
Roberts, (Uriah)	x													
01 Roberts, W. Jonah			x											
09 Roberts. William										x				
02 Roberts, Zariah														
02 Robertson, Allexander			x	x	x		x			x		x	x	
01 Robeson, Abraham			x											
10 Robertson, C.											x			
10 Robertson, David											x			
Robertson, James	x	x	x	x	x		x			x	x		x	1-Robeson
09 Robertson, John										x				
01 Robeson, Joseph			x											
Robertson, Richard	x													
Robertson, Samuel	x	x	x	x	x	x	x			x	x		x	1-Robeson
04 Robertson, Samuel						x								
01 Rolsten, Samuel			x	x										(Rawlings) ?
06 Roseberry, Hugh							x			x				
07 Ross, Adam									x					
09 Ross, Allexander											x	x	x	
05 Rowlis, William						x								
10 Rozier, Adam											x			
Rubey, Joseph	x	x												1-Ruby
04 Ruby, Samuel					x									
02 Ruddle, William			x	x										see Riddle
10 Runels, Michael											x			

Person	18 00	01	02	03	04	05	06	07	08	09	10	11	
09 S's - 7 unknown													
10 Sadler, Edward											x	x	
Sadler, John	x	x	x	x	x	x	x		x	x	x	x	9-Sater
04 Sample, George					x								
10 Sample, Mary											x		
Sample, Robert	x	x		x									
Sanders, Fitzhugh	x												
01 Sanders, Hezekiah		x	x	x	x	x						x	4-Sau
Sanders, James	x		x	x	x	x			x			x	4-Saunders
04 Saunders, William					x	x	x						
01 Sanderson, James		x											
09 Sanderson, John										x		x	
Sanderson, John	x	x	x	x	x	x	x		x				5-Sr.
Sanderson, John, Jr.	x	x	x	x	x	x							
10 Sanderson, Mary											x		
06 Sanderson, Robert							x		x		x		
09 Sater, John										x		x	
10 Savatier, William											x		
Scott, Adam	x												
06 Scott, Andrew							x		x	x	x	x	
Scott, Gabriel	x	x		x									
Scott, John	x	x	x	x	x	x			x	x	x	x	2-Seat
03 Scott, Jossiah				x		x							
Scott, Mathew	x	x	x	x	x	x		x		x	x	x	2-Seat
Scott, Moses	x	x	x	x	x	x							2-Seat
04 Scott, P. James					x	x							
Scott, Thomas	x	x	x	x	x	x	x	x	x	x	x	x	2-Seat
Scott, Thomas (0a)	x	x			x	x			x	x	x	x	8-Jr.
09 Scott, Thomas, Sr.										x	x		
Scott, Solomon	x	x	x	x	x	x							2-Seat
03 Scott, William				x									
10 Selby, Isaac											x	x	
01 Seldon, Roger		x											
10 Shankfort, Agnes											x		
11 Shankland, David												x	
09 Shankland, James										x	x		
Shankland, John	x	x	x	x	x	x	x		x	x	x	x	2-Shankling
06 Shanklin, John (6a)							x						
08 Shannon, John									x	x	x		
06 Shannon, Margaret							x		x	x	x	x	
01 Shannon, Samuel		x	x				x		x			x	

Person	00	01	02	03	04	05	06	07	08	09	10	11	
Shannon, Thomas	x	x	x	x	x	x							
08 Sharp, John (T.)									x	x	x	x	9-Shaps
11 Short, George												x	
Shaw, Henry	x												
Shaw, John	x	x	x	x	x								
Shaw, William	x	x		x	x								
01 Shepherd, John		x	x	x				x		x			1-Sheepherd
Shields, William	x		x										
Shillinger, Adam	x	x	x	x	x	x	x		x	x			
Shively, John	x	x											
02 Sloop, Joseph			x	x	x	x		x		x	x	x	
10 Smalley, John											x	x	
11 Smart, Humphrey												x	
Smart, Joseph	x		x	x		x							
02 Smart, Samuel			x			x							
09 Smith, Abrah										x	x	x	11-Absolum
03 Smith, David				x	x	x	x		x	x		x	
05 Smith, Elijah						x							
09 Smith, Ezekiel										x			
10 Smith, Gus											x		
07 Smith, Hezekiah								x			x	x	
08 Smith, Hugh									x	x	x		
05 Smith, James						x		x				x	
05 Smith, James (5a)						x							
Smith, John	x	x				x			x	x	x	x	
08 Smith, John (8a)									x			x	
06 Smith, Mitchel							x		x		x	x	
03 Smith, Nathan				x	x	x							
Smith, William	x	x		x	x	x		x		x	x	x	
09 Snap, Daniel										x		x	
Snap, George	x	x		x	x	x	x		x		x	x	5-Sr.
03 Snap, George (3a)				x	x	x							5-Jr.
01 Snap, John		x		x	x	x		x	x			x	
Snap, Peter	x	x	x	x	x	x	x		x	x	x	x	
09 Snap, Samuel										x	x	x	
06 Snortgrass, John							x		x				8-Snodgrass
06 Sparks, George							x		x				
Sparks, Joseph	x												
01 Spaw, Henry		x	x	x	x	x	x	x		x	x		3-Spaugh 4-Sporr
07 Spaw, Jacob								x		x	x	x	
06 Sowsly, George David							x						

Person	18 00	01	02	03	04	05	06	07	08	09	10	11	
Standiford, Aquila	x	x	x	x	x	x				x		x	2-Equalay 9Quilly
Standiford, Elijah	x	x	x	x	x	x							
01 Sandiford, George		x	x	x	x	x		x		x	x	x	2-St
11 Standeford, James												x	
09 Standeford, John										x		x	
Sandiford, Nathan	x	x	x	x									2-St 3Standerford
07 Standiford, Sarah								x			x		
09 Star, Hollidy										x			
11 Steel, Hugh												x	
08 Steals, James								x			x		8-Stears
11 Steals, John												x	
11 Steel, Joseph												x	
04 Steel, William				x	x			x			x		8-Stears
04 Steel, William, Jr.				x	x								
02 Steven, Charles			x										
05 Stephenson, Alexander					x								
10 Stephenson, Eliza										x	x		11-Betsy
Stephenson, (Havers)	x												
Stephenson, James	x	x	x	x	x	x	x			x			
02 Stevenson, Joseph		x	x	x		x				x	x	x	
01 Stephenson, (Marow)		x	x	x	x	x							2-Mark 3-Marhas
Stephenson, Robert	x	x		x	x		x			x	x		
09 Stephenson, Robert, Jr.										x	x	x	
Stephenson, Thomas	x	x	x	x	x	x		x		x	x	x	2-Stevenson
Stephenson, William	x	x		x	x	x				x		x	
03 Stuart, Charles			x	x	x								
Stewart, James	x	x		x	x							x	
Stewart, John	x	x		x	x								
Stewart, Joseph	x	x	x	x	x	x		x		x	x	x	
06 Stewart, Mary							x		x		x	x	
Stewart, Mathew	x	x	x	x		x		x					
Stewart, Robert	x			x									
03 Stuart, William				x									
Stewart, Williby('oughby)	x	x	x	x	x	x		x		x	x	x	3-Stuart
08 Stinson, James									x				
08 Stinson, Joseph									x				
02 Stinson, Robert			x										
06 Stinson, William						x		x					
06 Stockwell, Ann						x							
01 Stockdel, James		x			x	x							4-Stockdale
06 Stockwell, John						x			x	x	x	x	

Person	18	00	01	02	03	04	05	06	07	08	09	10	11	
06 Stockwell, Michael								x						
05 Stockdell, William							x	x						6-Stockwell
02 Stogdel, James			x	x					x		x	x	x	7-Stogdale
03 Stogal, William				x					x		x	x	x	
01 Stoop, George		x												
Stoops, Phillip	x		x	x	x	x	x		x	x	x	x		
02 Stotts, Addam			x											
02 Stovall, Jess			x											
Stubs, Anny	x	x	x											
07 Suiter, John									x					
10 Surs, John											x			
07 Swain, Nathan									x		x	x	x	
10 Swanson, John											x			
10 Swanson, John (10a)											x			
Swarts, James	x		x		x	x			x		x	x		
10 Swart, H.											x			
Sworden, Quinten	x	x	x	x	x	x								2-Sorden
Sumet, Christian	x	x	x	x	x	x	x		x	x	x	x		3-Summit-Summersett
Sumet, George	x	x	x	x		x	x		x	x	x	x		3-Summit-Summersett
08 Summerfield, Richard									x	x	x	x		10 -'veal 11'sett
06 Suddoth, Francis							x		x					
05 Sutton, Ebenzer						x	x		x		x			5-Shuttan
09 Sutton, Elizabeth										x				
05 Sutton, John						x	x		x		x			5 Shuttan
04 Shuttan, William					x	x								
04 Swayhey, John					x									

Person	18 00	01	02	03	04	05	06	07	08	09	10	11	
09 T's - 1 unknown													
10 T----, Titus											x		
Tanner, James	x		x										
11 Tarvar, George												x	
02 Tasley, John			x										
Tate, Francis	x	x	x	x		x		x					
01 Tate, James		x											
03 Taylor, George				x				x	x	x	x	x	
09 Taylor, George (9a)										x	x	x	
Taylor, James	x	x	x	x		x							2-Talor
02 Taylor, John			x	x	x	x		x		x	x	x	2-Talor 11-Sr.
11 Taylor, John, Jr.											x		
01 Taylor, Joseph		x											
02 Tayler, Joshua			x	x	x	x	x		x	x	x		
02 Talor, Josias			x	x	x	x		x					3-Taylor
Taylor, Leason John	x	x											
03 Taylor, Nathaniel			x	x	x		x			x	x	x	
09 Taylor, Richard										x			
09 Taylor, Tapley										x	x	x	
Taylor, Thomas	x	x	x	x	x	x							2-Talor
Taylor, Thomas (0a)	x	x	x	x									2-Talor
Taylor, William	x	x	x	x	x								
Taylor, William (0a)	x												
02 Thardgal, William			x										
Thomas, Edward	x	x	x	x	x	x	x		x	x	x	x	
Thompson, Anthony	x												
Thompson, Alexander	x	x	x	x	x	x	x		x	x	x		
08 Thompson, Daniel									x	x	x	x	
Thompson, Henry	x	x	x	x	x	x	x		x	x		x	1-Thomson 11-Sr.
04 Thomson, H. James				x	x	x				x		x	
03 Thompson, James			x	x	x				x		x	x	5-Sr.
Thompson, James, Jr.	x	x	x	x									
Thompson, Joseph	x	x	x	x	x	x						x	11-Joshua
08 Thompson, Moses									x				
07 Thompson, Nathan								x					
03 Thompson, Reuben			x										
06 Thompson, Sarah							x			x	x	x	
11 Thompson, Susannah												x	
11 Thompson, Samuel												x	
Thompson, Thomas	x		x										
Thompson, William	x	x		x	x	x	x		x	x	x	x	

Person	1800	01	02	03	04	05	06	07	08	09	10	11	
10 Thornton, Anthony											x	x	
10 Throckmorton, Ari											x	x	11-Ariss
02 Throckmorton, John			x	x	x	x		x		x	x	x	7/9-Thogmorton
Throckmorton, Thomas	x	x	x	x	x	x		x		x	x	x	0-listed Morton
01 Throckmorton, Th.,Jr.		x		x	x	x		x		x	x	x	
10 Tomkins, K.											x		10(Kinsnit ?)
Toppins, Robert	x	x		x	x	x							
09 Towhair, Nathan										x			see Crowheir
Towler													see Fowler
10 Trulove, Will C.											x	x	
Trousdale, John	x	x											
Trousdale, William	x	x	x										02-Thardgal
Tully, John	x	x		x	x								
04 Turnbull, John					x	x							
Ungles													see Ingles

Person	1800	01	02	03	04	05	06	07	08	09	10	11	
02 Vancriff, Elizabeth		x	x										see Montcrief
01 Vanhook, Abner		x		x	x	x		x			x	x	
01 Vanhook, Archiles		x		x	x	x		x			x	x	4-Archibald 7 'helaus
01 Vanhook, Martin			x	x									
03 Vanhook, Samuel				x		x		x			x	x	
06 Vanskike, Hezekiah							x		x	x	x	x	
01 Varner, Koonrod	x												
Vaughn, Daniel	x	x	x	x	x	x							2-Vaun
10 Vaugh, Jacob										x			
10 Vaugh, Jacob (10a)										x			
Vaughn, Thomas	x	x	x	x	x	x	x		x	x	x	x	2-Vaun -3 Vawn
01 Veach, John		x	x	x									3-Veatch
Vennoy, Francis	x	x	x	x	x	x					x	x	10-Bernoy
04 Verden, Hugh					x	x		x		x	x	x	7-Vurden
02 Vinegner, Richard			x										

Person	18	00	01	02	03	04	05	06	07	08	09	10	11	
Waggoner, Christian		x	x	x	x	x	x			x		x	x	5-Christopher
Waggoner, John		x	x	x	x	x	x		x		x	x	x	
10 Wates, Charles												x		
Waits, John		x	x	x	x	x	x		x			x		4/5-Wales 7Wiets
Wallace, William		x	x	x	x	x	x		x		x	x	x	2-Wallis
02 Wallis, William				x										
Ward, Andrew		x	x											
Ward, George		x	x											
Ward, Thomas		x												
10 Warren, Isaac												x	x	11-Warrant
11 Waterford, Benjamin													x	
Watson, James		x	x	x	x	x	x		x		x	x	x	
03 Watson, James, Jr.					x	x	x		x		x	x		
11 Watson, Patrick													x	
Waugh, George		x												
07 Waugh, Jacob									x		x		x	
Waugh, Samuel (M.)		x	x	x	x	x	x	x		x			x	
Weaver, William		x	x	x										
Webb, Anny		x	x		x	x	x							
03 Web, Charles					x		x				x		x	11-Webb
03 Web, Eli					x									
Webb, William		x	x											
09 Webster, Daniel											x			
04 Webster, Mary					x									
06 Webster, Nathan							x						x	11-Nathaniel
01 Wesbter, Sires(Tobias)			x	x	x									3-Cyrus
Welch, Abraham		x	x	x	x									2-Walch
03 Wells, Aaron					x			x			x	x		Wells/Wills
10 Wills, Charles											x			
10 Wills, David											x			
Wills, John		x	x	x	x			x		x	x	x	x	Wills/Wells
03 Wills, John					x									
10 Wells, Nathan												x	x	
West, Amos		x	x	x	x	x	x	x		x	x	x	x	
03 West, Eli					x		x	x			x		x	9-Elijah
09 West, John											x	x	x	
09 West, John (9a)											x	x		
West, Isaac		x	x	x	x	x	x	x		x	x		x	
09 West, Philip											x	x	x	
West, Thomas		x		x	x	x			x		x	x	x	
10 West, Thomas (10a)											x			

Person	18	00	01	02	03	04	05	06	07	08	09	10	11	Notes
02 Whally, William				x										
Wheeler, William		x	x		x		x	x		x		x	x	
09 Whitaker, James											x	x	x	
05 White, John							x	x			x	x	x	
09 Whitecotton, Moses											x			
09 Whitely, David											x	x	x	10-Daniel
09 Whitly, William											x	x	x	
07 Whitney, John									x					
05 Wiggons, Aaron							x							
Wiggons, John		x	x	x	x	x	x		x		x	x	x	2-Wigon
07 Wiggons, William									x		x	x	x	9-Wiggins
05 Wiley, Aaron							x							
05 Whilley, Daniel							x	x						
05 Wiley, Hugh							x			x	x	x	x	
Wiley, John		x		x		x	x	x		x		x	x	2-Wile 6-Sr.
06 Wiley, John, Jr.								x		x	x	x	x	
09 Wiley, Johnson											x			
Wiley, Samuel		x		x	x	x	x			x	x	x	x	
04 Wiley, William						x	x	x		x	x		x	
09 Williamson, James											x			
03 Williamson, John					x	x	x					x	x	
Williams, Hubbard		x	x											
Williams, John		x	x	x	x	x	x	x		x	x	x	x	
02 Williams, John (2a)				x										
02 Williams, Nathan				x	x	x								4-Nathaniel
09 Williams, William											x	x	x	
11 Williams, William (11a)													x	
Wills														see Wells
Wilson, Benjamin		x	x	x	x	x		x			x	x	x	1-Willon
Willson, Benjamin		x	x		x									
08 Wilson, Charles										x	x		x	
09 Wilson, Isaac											x	x	x	
05 Wilson, James							x		x			x	x	
10 Wilson, James (10a)												x		
10 Wilson, Jane												x		
06 Wilson, John								x				x		
02 Wilson, Robert				x								x		
05 Wilson, Thomas							x							
Wisely, William		x	x											
07 Wiseman, Hitch									x		x			7- Wise Hitch
Wishard, William		x												

Person	18	00	01	02	03	04	05	06	07	08	09	10	11	
02 Woolf, John				x	x									
Wolf, Joseph		x	x	x	x									2-Woolf
10 Woolen, Leonard												x	x	
09 Woolens, William											x	x	x	
Wood, John		x												
06 Wood, Robert								x						
10 Wood, Hilkiah												x	x	
09 Worain, Isaac											x			
11 Wright, Charles													x	
11 Wright, John													x	

Person	18	00	01	02	03	04	05	06	07	08	09	10	11
04 Yates, Andrew					x					x	x	x	x
04 Yates, William					x						x		
03 Young, Allexander					x		x				x	x	x
Young, Jacob		x			x	x	x	x		x	x	x	x
07 Young, John									x				
Young, William		x											

Free Negroes
(xx out)

Person	18	00	01	02	03
Black Joe					x
Richard Black					x
John Hannah					x

*1810 CENSUS ADDITIONS
------Only listed 1810   USING TAX LISTS

Person	18 00	01	02	03	04	05	06	07	08	09	10	11	
04 Alexander, Jesse					x	x	x		x	x	x		
10 Alexander, Thomas											x	x	
Allen, William	x	x	x	x		x	x			x	x	x	
05 Allen, William, Jr.						x	x				x	x	
04 Allfrey, James					x	x	x		x		x		
Allison, Alexander	x	x	x	x		x		x		x	x	x	2-Alb---h, xanpe
Allison, John	x	x	x	x	x	x		x		x	x	x	
03 Anderson, Daniel			x	x	x	x		x		x	x		
10 Anderson, Edward											x	x	
Anderson, George	x	x	x	x	x	x	x		x	x	x	x	8-Sr.
Anderson, John	x	x	x	x						x	x	x	
10 Anderson, Richard										x—----------			
10 Anderson, Sarah											x	x	
02 Archer, James			x	x	x		x		x		x	x	
Archer, John	x	x	x	x	x	x	x		x	x	x	x	5-Sr.
04 Archer, John					x	x	x		x	x	x	x	5-Jr.
02 Archer, Sampson			x	x	x		x		x	x	x	x	
Ardery, James	x	x		x	x	x	x		x		x	x	
09 Ardery, Robert										x	x	x	
10 Armstrong, Irvin											x	x	
Arnett, Samuel	x	x		x	x	x	x		x	x	x	x	0-ot 5Arneth 6Arnet
Arnold, Lewis H.	x	x	x	x	x	x					x	x	
10 Artt, James											x	x	
02 Art, Thomas			x	x							x	x	
Art, William	x	x	x	x	x	x		x		x	x	x	
01 Art, William, Jr.		x	x		x					x	x	x	
07 Asberry, Henry								x		x	x	x	
03 Asberry, William				x	x	x		x		x	x	x	
03 Asberry, William, Jr.				x	x	x		x		x	x	x	
02 Ashcraft, Ephraim			x	x	x	x			x	x	x	x	
Ashcraft, Jacob	x	x	x	x	x	x				x	x	x	
10 Ashley, James											x	x	
B													
01 Bailey, Basel		x	x	x	x	x		x		x	x	x	3-Bayley 10 Baley
Bailey, John	x	x	x	x	x	x	x		x		x		6-Bayley
08 Baker, Jacob									x		x	x	
Baker, James	x	x						x		x	x	x	
07 Baker, John								x		x	x	x	
09 Baker, John (9a)										x	x		

Person	1800	01	02	03	04	05	06	07	08	09	10	11	
Baker, Martin	x	x	x	x	x					x	x	x	
Baker, William	x	x	x	x	x	x		x			x	x	
Ballingall, David	x	x	x	x	x	x		x		x	x	x	7-Benin' 9Bedin'
10 Ballenger, William											x	x	
04 Barlow, Jesse				x	x	x		x			x	x	
Barlow, John	x	x		x	x	x	x		x	x	x	x	10 Barwell
Barlow, William	x	x	x	x	x	x	x		x	x	x	x	
Barnet, Ambrose	x	x	x	x	x	x	x		x	x	x	x	
05 Barnet, John						x	x		x	x	x	x	
05 Barnet, William						x	x		x	x	x	x	5/7/10-Burnet
10 Bartlett, (Cenna)										x			
Bartlett, Ebenzer	x	x	x	x		x		x		x	x	x	
09 Bartlett, Joseph										x	x	x	
Bartlett, Samuel	x	x	x	x		x				x	x	x	
Bartlett, William	x	x	x	x	x	x		x		x	x	x	
Basket, Jesse	x	x	x	x	x	x	x		x	x	x	x	
10 Barwell, John										x			
03 Beaty, John				x	x	x					x	x	5-Beasnt 10'ton 11'ter
Bedinger, George M.	x	x	x	x				x		x	x		
03 Bell, Jane				x	x	x	x				x	x	
10 Bell, Jane (10a)											x	x	
*Bennington, Nehemiah	x	x	x	x	x	x	x		x	x		x	
Bentley, Michael	x	x	x	x		x					x	x	
Berry, Robert	x		x	x	x	x	x		x		x	x	
10 Blackburn, Julius H.											x	x	
Blair, Alexander	x	x	x	x		x	x		x		x	x	
10 Blair, Sarah										x			
10 Blastengun, William										x			
*02 Blunt, Reading			x	x		x	x					x	11-Blount
Boatman, Henry	x	x							x	x	x	x	9-Boteman
03 Bogges, Thomas				x	x	x		x		x	x	x	3-Bogus
09 Boles, John						x		x	x	x	x		5-Bowles 9-Bales
Bolen, William	x	x		x	x						x	x	3- Bowlin 10-Boles
03 Bossley, Bennidick				x	x	x	x		x		x		10 Benax
10 Boswell, William										x			
Bowen, William	x		x	x		x			x	x	x	x	
Boyd, John	x	x	x	x	x	x	x		x		x	x	6-Boid
10 Boyd, John (10a)										x			
07 Bradly, Daniel								x		x			
07 Bradly, George								x		x	x	x	9-Brady
09 Bradly, Robert										x	x	x	

Person	1800	01	02	03	04	05	06	07	08	09	10	11	
09 Bradshaw, David										x	x	x	
10 Branen, James										x-————10 Broren			
09 Branon, John										x	x		
10 Brinton, Eliza										x-————			
10 Brinton, James										x	x		
10 Brinson, John										x-————			
Brinson, Jonathan	x			x						x	x	x	3-Brunson 9 Brinton
*05 Brinton, Robert					x					x		x	9-Brinton 11 Brenton
Brinson, Thomas	x	x	x	x	x	x			x	x	x	x	3-Brunson 11-Sr.
09 Brooks, Susanna										x	x		10-Hannah
08 Brooks, Zachariah									x		x	x	
*03 Brown, Allexander			x	x	x				x	x		x	
*02 Brown, David			x	x	x	x	x		x			x	11-Sr.
Brown, James	x	x	x	x	x				x	x	x	x	
03 Brown, James (3a)				x	x				x	x			
Brown, John	x	x		x	x	x	x	x	x		x	x	
03 Brown, John (3a)				x	x	x	x		x		x	x	
*09 Brown, John (9a)										x		x	
05 Brown, Parker						x					x	x	5-Larkin
08, Brown, William									x		x	x	
07 Buchannon, Phebe								x		x	x	x	
*09 Buckler, Robert										x		x	
02 Bucklor, Stephen			x	x							x	x	
06 Buckner, Henry							x		x		x	x	11-Harry
03 Buckner, Samuel				x	x	x	x		x		x	x	
08 Bunton, Andrew									x		x	x	
10 Bunton, Charles											x	x	
02 Bunton, James	x	x	x	x	x	x	x		x		x	x	0/1-Benton
02 Bunton, John	x	x	x	x	x	x	x		x		x		0/1-Benton
10 Bunton, Josiah											x-————		
02 Bunton, William	x	x	x	x	x	x	x		x		x	x	01/-Benton
02 Burns, John			x	x				x			x		
*02 Burius, John			x		x	x	x					x	5-Burrus
02 Burrius, John			x			x			x		x	x	8 Burrows
*09 Busby, Archibald										x		x	
10 Busby, Mathew											x	x	
02 Busby, William			x	x	x	x			x		x	x	3-Bazby
Byers, David	x	x	x	x	x	x	x		x		x	x	
10 Byers, John											x	x	
08 Byrum, Agustus									x	x	x	x	9-Bryam

Person	18 00	01	02	03	04	05	06	07	08	09	10	11	
C													
Caldwell, Alexander	x	x	x	x	x	x	x		x		x	x	
Caldwell, David	x	x	x	x	x	x	x		x	x	x	x	6-Sr.
Caldwell, David (0a)	x	x	x		x	x	x		x		x	x	
Caldwell, Robert	x	x	x	x	x	x	x		x	x	x	x	
02 Caldwell, Robert (2a)		x		x	x	x					x	x	
*Caldwell, Robert, Jr.	x		x	x					x			x	
03 Caldwell, Thomas			x	x	x	x			x	x	x	x	
10 Caldwell, Thomas (10a)											x-------		
05 Caldwell, Walter					x	x			x	x	x		
Caldwell, William	x	x	x	x	x	x	x	x	x		x	x	7-McCadwell
*Caldwell, William (0a)	x	x	x	x	x	x					x		
10 Camerett, George											x-------		
*Cameron, Samuel	x	x	x	x	x	x		x			x		
10 Campbell, Daniel											x	x	
*Campbell, James	x	x	x	x	x	x	x		x	x		x	0/1-Campble
04 Campbell, John					x		x				x	x	
Campbell, Jossias	x	x	x	x	x		x		x		x	x	0/1Campble 11Jonas
10 Campbell, Samuel											x-------		
04 Carabough, Peter				x	x		x				x		6-Carrabough
Carothers, Thomas	x	x	x	x	x	x		x		x	x	x	9-Carthers
03 Carnahan, James			x		x	x			x	x	x	x	6-Sr.
03 Carnahan, James (3a)			x			x			x	x	x	x	6-Jr.
04 Carnahan, Robert				x	x	x			x	x	x	x	
09 Carter, Daniel										x	x	x	
01 Carter, Jonathan		x								x	x		
Casey, James	x		x	x			x			x	x		9-Kasey10Casesey
08 Casey, John									x		x	x	10-Casesey
Cassidy, Daniel	x	x	x	x	x	x	x		x	x	x	x	
01 Cassady, James		x	x	x	x	x	x		x	x	x	x	
08 Cassady, Jeremiah									x		x		
*Catherwood, Charles	x	x	x	x		x		x		x		x	7/9-Ketherwood
10 Catherwood, John											x-------		
Catherwood, Samuel	x			x	x	x	x	x		x	x	x	7/9-Ketherwood
10 Caughey, David											x	x	
Caughey, John	x	x	x	x	x	x	x				x	x	
10 Chaney, James										x	x		
08 Chaney, John									x		x		
10 Chaney, John (10a)											x-------		
06 Chaney, William							x		x		x	x	
09 Clark, Benjamin										x	x	x	

Person	18 00	01	02	03	04	05	06	07	08	09	10	11	
10 Clark, Benjamin (10a)											x	x	
04 Clarke, David					x	x	x	x			x	x	
Clark, John	x							x		x	x	x	9-Sr.
04 Clarke, William					x	x				x	x	x	
*08 Clay, Thomas									x			x	
07 Clay, William								x		x	x	x	11-Sr.
10 Cochran, Margaret											x-----		
Collier, A. Coleman	x	x		x		x					x		3-reversed
02 Collier, Clairburn			x	x		x				x	x	x	3- reversed
*03 Collier, Franklin				x	x	x	x			x		x	
Collier, Hamlet	x					x	x			x	x	x	
Collier, John	x	x	x	x	x	x	x				x	x	
02 Collins, Edmund			x	x	x	x	x				x	x	
09 Collings, Stephen										x	x	x	
Conway, John	x	x		x	x	x	x			x	x		
05 Cook, John						x			x		x		
10 Cook, Peter											x	x	
10 Cooper, John											x	x	
02 Corbin, Abraham			x	x	x	x	x		x		x	x	
10 Cord, Ashary											x-----		
07 Cosby, Overton								x			x	x	
Cottrel, Thomas	x		x	x	x		x		x	x	x	x	
Cowan, Issac	x	x	x	x	x	x	x		x	x	x	x	2-Cowin 9-Cororn
*Cowan, John	x	x	x	x	x	x						x	
*06 Crawford, Mary						x	x		x			x	
Crawford, Samuel	x	x	x	x	x	x		x		x	x	x	
08 Crawford, William									x	x	x		
07 Culp, James								x			x		7-Clup
09 Culp, Thomas										x	x		9-Clup
D													
05 Dailey, Mary						x		x		x	x		9-Dagley
01 Dailey, John S.		x			x	x		x		x	x	x	9-Daisey
05 Darland, Abraham					x	x		x	x	x	x	x	9-Darling
Davidson, John	x	x				x	x		x	x	x	x	
*Davidson, Thomas	x	x	x		x	x	x		x	x		x	
Davis, Robert	x	x	x	x	x	x		x		x	x	x	
03 Davis, Thomas				x		x				x	x	x	
10 Davis, Thomas (10a)											x-----		
02 Davis, William			x	x	x	x				x	x	x	
03 Davis, William (3a)				x		x					x		5-Jr.
Dayton, Garret	x	x	x	x	x	x	x		x	x	x	x	0/1-Dalton 8 Deyton

119

Person	1800	01	02	03	04	05	06	07	08	09	10	11	
Deal, Mathew	x	x	x	x			x		x	x	x	x	9-Dial
10 Deen, Abraham										x------			
09 Demitt, Henry										x	x	x	9-Dmitt 10Dew'
08 Dickey, Alexander									x		x		
06 Dingle, William							x		x	x	x	x	
Dils, Abraham	x	x	x	x	x				x		x	x	4Dilce 5Dilts 8 Dill
09 Dinsmore, James										x	x		
Dinsmore, Henry	x	x	x	x	x	x	x		x	x	x	x	0/1-Dinsmer
*Dinsmore, John	x		x	x		x	x		x	x		x	0/1-Dinsmer
06 Dorough, James							x				x	x	10 Dorrow
10 Dotson, Dennis										x------			
08 Dotson, James									x	x	x	x	9-Datson
10 Doson, William										x------			
10 Dougherty, James										x	x		
07 Douhety, Jesse								x		x	x	x	10-Daugherty
06 Doughty, John							x		x	x	x	x	10 Dougherty
10 Doughty, Thomas									x	x	x		
06 Doughty, William							x		x	x	x		
Downey, Arch.	x	x	x	x	x	x	x		x		x	x	2/3-Downing
Drummond, James	x	x	x	x	x	x	x		x		x	x	0/1-Drumins
10 Dun, Abraham										x------			
11 Duncon, Archibald										x	x		
03 Duncan, James			x	x	x		x		x	x	x		
01 Dunkon, Joseph		x	x	x	x	x		x	x	x	x		2/3-Duncan
02 Duncan, William			x	x	x	x		x		x	x		
Duzan, Jacob	x	x		x	x	x		x		x	x	x	3-Druzan
03 Druzan, William			x		x			x	x	x	x		5-Duzan
E													
*Earlywine, Daniel	x	x	x	x	x	x	x		x	x		x	2/3/4/5-Arelywine
Earlywine, George	x	x	x	x	x	x	x		x	x	x	x	2/3/4/5-Arelywine
08 Earlywine, Jacob									x	x	x	x	
10 Earlywine, Samuel										x------			
01 Easely, Joseph		x		x						x			3-Jossah
10 Eaton, Jacob										x	x		
09 Edwards, Hannah										x	x	x	10-Harriet
09 Ellerback, John										x	x	x	
Ellis, John	x	x	x	x	x	x		x		x	x	x	
Ellis, James	x	x	x	x	x	x	x		x	x	x	x	6-Sr.
06 Ellis, James, Jr.							x		x		x	x	
*09 Ellis, William										x		x	
Enlow, Jesse	x	x	x	x	x	x	x		x	x	x	x	2/3/6/10-Inlow

Person	1800	01	02	03	04	05	06	07	08	09	10	11	
*08 Eslick, Joseph									x			x	11-Earlick
02 Estes, Thomas			x	x	x	x		x		x	x	x	10/11-Eastes
*02 Evans, John			x	x	x	x		x		x			x	8-Evins
10 Eavins, Rachel											x---------		
F													
10 Farmer, Charles											x---------		
Fearman, John	x	x		x	x	x		x			x	x	
02 Feeback, Frederick			x	x	x	x				x	x		
Ferren, Hugh	x		x		x	x	x		x		x		(McFerren) 10 Fern
09 Fielder, George										x	x	x	
01 Fields, Ebenzer		x	x	x	x	x		x		x	x	x	11-Fellies
05, Fields, William						x		x		x	x	x	11-Feelas
02 Fight, Jacob			x	x	x	x	x		x	x	x	x	
09 Fitzpatrick, James										x	x	x	
Forsyth, John	x	x	x	x	x	x	x		x		x	x	
07 Foster, Harrison								x		x	x		
10 Foster, Rhode											x----------		
02 Fowler, James			x			x				x	x	x	
Fowler, Luke	x	x	x	x		x			x	x	x	x	(listed in T's)
Frazer, James	x	x	x		x	x	x		x		x		5-Frazier
Frazer, William	x	x	x	x	x	x		x			x		5-Sr.
10 Fry, John										x	x		
01 Fryman, George		x	x		x	x	x		x	x		x	4-Friman
10 Fryman, Henry										x	x		
Fryman, Phillip	x	x	x		x	x		x		x	x	x	
06 Fuller, Joseph							x		x	x	x	x	
*09 Fulton, John										x		x	
03 Fulton, Samuel				x		x	x			x	x	x	
G													
10 Gadman, William											x--------		
*Gamble, David	x	x	x	x	x	x	x	x		x		x	
*04 Gaffen, Oath					x	x	x					x	
Galbreath, Benjamin	x	x	x	x	x	x	x		x	x	x	x	2-Jalbreath 8 Bal'
Galbreath, William	x	x	x	x	x	x	x		x	x	x		2-Jalbreath
Gateral, Thomas ('rell)	x	x	x	x		x		x		x			0-Gattinel 3-Gatingel
Geoghegan, John	x	x	x	x	x	x	x			x	x	x	0-Goehegan
08 Geoghegan, John, Jr.									x	x	x	x	
*02 Geoghegan, Michael			x	x	x	x	x					x	
04 Gillaspie, James					x		x			x	x	x	6-Gallaspe
Githens, Henry	x	x	x	x	x	x	x		x	x	x	x	0/1Gidions 2Geathens
Githens, James	x	x		x	x	x	x		x	x	x		0/1Gidions 9Gwaithin

Person	1800	01	02	03	04	05	06	07	08	09	10	11	
Githens, John	x	x	x	x	x	x			x		x	x	0/1Gidions 2 Gthens
10 Glasscock, Cena											x--------		
10 Glasscock, Peggy											x--------		
*Glassgow, James	x	x		x								x	
09 Glen, Simone										x	x		
10 Godsey, Gilbert											x--------		
Gonce, George	x	x	x		x	x	x			x	x	x	x	2-Gones
Gonce, Nicholas	x	x			x	x	x			x	x	x	x	6-Gaunce
02 Gonsollus, James			x	x	x	x					x	x	3-Gunsaullus
10 Gonsallas, Thomas											x	x	
08 Gorman, Daniel									x	x	x	x	
09-Gragg, Joseph										x	x	x	
02 Graham, James			x	x	x	x	x			x		x	x	
Gray, David	x	x	x	x	x	x		x	x	x	x	x	2-Grey
Gray, David (0a)	x	x		x	x	x				x	x	x	11-Jr.
01 Gray, James		x	x	x	x	x	x				x	x	
09 Gray, Isaac										x	x	x	11-Sr.
09 Green, Zachariah										x	x		
Griffin, Gabriel	x	x		x	x	x		x			x	x	
05 Griffith, Martin						x			x	x	x	x	
Grosvener, Richard	x	x		x	x	x		x		x	x	x	0'Grossowmer3 'vines
H													
06 Hains, George						x	x			x	x		10/11-Hanes
Hall, Benjamin	x	x	x	x	x	x	x		x	x	x	x	
Hall, Cornelius	x	x	x	x	x	x	x		x	x	x	x	
*09 Hall, Elihu										x		x	
Hall, James	x	x	x	x		x			x	x	x	x	
Hall, Moses	x	x	x	x	x	x	x		x	x	x	x	
02 Hall, Robert			x	x	x	x	x		x	x	x	x	
09 Hall, Samuel										x	x	x	
02 Hall, William			x	x	x	x	x		x	x	x	x	
*02 Hamilton, James			x	x	x	x	x	x				x	2-Hammelton
Hamilton, John	x	x	x	x	x	x	x		x	x	x	x	2-Hammelton
02 Hamilton, Thomas			x		x						x		2- Hammelton
Harden, Elihu	x	x	x	x	x	x		x		x	x	x	
02 Harden, John			x	x	x			x		x	x		9-Hardik
Harney, Hiram	x	x	x	x	x	x		x		x	x	x	
Harney, Mills	x	x	x	x	x	x		x		x	x	x	
Harney, Rollen	x	x	x	x	x	x		x		x	x	x	
02 Harney, Thomas			x	x	x	x		x		x	x	x	
10 Hartley, Elizabeth											x--------		

122

Person	18	00	01	02	03	04	05	06	07	08	09	10	11	
08 Hartley, Mordicai										x	x		x	
10 Hartsock, Samuel												x–––––––––		
06 Haslet, Samuel								x			x	x	x	
Hawkins, Samuel		x	x	x		x	x			x	x	x	x	
Hawkins, Thomas		x	x	x	x		x	x		x	x	x	x	
Helpman, John		x	x	x		x	x			x	x			9-Helpenson
10 Henry, John											x	x		
08 Herbert, William										x		x	x	10/11-Harbert
07 Hiatt, Shadrack									x			x	x	10/11-Hyatt
Hildreth, Squire		x	x		x	x	x		x		x	x	x	1-Hildridge
Hill, James		x	x	x	x	x	x	x		x	x	x	x	
Hill, John		x	x	x	x	x	x	x		x	x	x		
*06 Hill, Richard								x			x		x	
10 Hillick, (Alvin)												x–––––––––		
02 Hinton, Ezekiel			x	x		x	x			x	x	x	x	
07 Hitch, Wise									x		x			see Wiseman
Holladay, William (i)		x	x	x		x	x	x		x	x	x		8 Holy'
10 Holler, Francis											x			
*07 Hollar, John									x		x		x	9-Holler
03 Holly, Thompson				x	x	x		x		x	x	x		4-Tom Hollow
03 Honical, Jacob				x	x	x		x		x	x	x		4-Honcan
09 Hopkins, Elihu										x	x			
10 (Hosen, Moshan)												x–––––––––		
*08 How, Ezra									x				x	
02 How, Samuel			x	x	x	x	x			x	x	x	x	5-Howe
Howard, Gidion	x				x	x				x	x	x	x	
10 Howard, Gidion (10a)											x	x		
06 Howard, Henry							x			x	x	x	x	
01 Howard, Jacob			x			x	x			x	x	x	x	
09 Howerton, George											x	x	x	
03 Huddleston, Allexander				x	x	x	x			x		x	x	5-Heddleston
*08 Hudson, Major										x			x	
10 Huffman, Abe												x–––––––––		
*Huffman, Peter		x	x	x	x	x	x	x		x	x		x	0/1-Hofman
Hughes, William		x	x		x	x	x			x	x	x	x	0/1-Hugh
Hunter, John		x	x	x		x	x		x		x	x		
I														
07 Ungles, John									x		x	x	x	listed in U's
07 Ingles, Peter									x		x	x		
06 Irvin, Andrew								x		x	x	x	x	
10 Irvin, George											x	x		

123

Person	18	00	01	02	03	04	05	06	07	08	09	10	11	
*05 Irvin, Samuel							x				x		x	
*04 Ishmail, James					x	x	x				x		x	
10 Ishmail, John												x	x	
08 Ishmail, Thomas										x		x	x	
J														
10 (Javinall), David												x	x	11-Juvinall
10 Jenkins, Mary											x--------			
*09 Jenkins, Thomas											x		x	
01 Johnston, Isom				x	x	x	x			x		x	x	
Johnston, James		x		x	x	x		x			x	x	x	9-Johnson
Johnston, James (0a)		x									x	x	x	
04 Johnson, John					x	x					x	x		
*Johnston, John Sr.		x	x	x	x	x	x	x		x	x		x	
10 Johnson, Joseph												x	x	
02 Johnston, Mason			x	x	x	x		x				x	x	11-Marion
02 Johnston, William			x	x	x	x	x			x	x	x		
Jolly, David		x	x	x	x	x	x	x		x	x	x		3-Golly
08 Jones, Drury										x	x	x	x	
Jones, Jacob		x	x	x	x	x	x	x	x	x	x	x	x	5-Sr.
*Jones, Jacob (0a)		x	x	x	x	x	x	x		x	x		x	5-Jr.
Jones, John		x	x	x	x	x	x	x		x	x	x		
Jones, Moses		x	x			x	x			x	x	x		
K														
07 Keath, Adam									x	x	x	x		
Keith, Jacob		x	x	x	x	x	x		x		x	x	x	7-Keath
Keith, Phillip		x	x	x	x	x	x		x		x	x	x	
04 Kelly, Thomas						x	x				x	x		
Kennedy, Andrew		x							x		x	x		
Kenedy, David		x				x		x		x	x	x		
06 Kennedy, Robert								x			x	x		
05 Kerns, Adam						x	x			x	x	x		10 Carns
*03 Kiles, John				x	x	x				x		x		9-Kite
Killgore, William		x	x	x	x	x	x			x	x	x	x	5-Gilgore
08 Kimbrough, Elizabeth										x	x	x	x	
Kimbrough, John		x	x		x	x	x		x		x	x	x	0/1-Kimbro
Kimbrough, Richard		x			x	x	x				x	x		0/1/2-Kimbro
07 Kimbrough, Robert									x		x	x	x	
02 Kincart, James				x	x	x		x		x	x	x	x	
08 Kincart, John										x	x	x	x	
Kincart, Samuel		x	x		x	x	x	x		x	x	x	x	
10 King, Barnett											x--------			

Person	1800	01	02	03	04	05	06	07	08	09	10	11	
09 Krusor, Michael										x	x	x	
L													
Leeper, John	x	x	x	x	x	x	x		x	x	x	x	8-Leaper
Lilly, Pleasant	x	x	x		x		x			x	x	x	3-xx out
02 Livingood, George	x	x	x	x	x	x		x		x	x	x	0/1-Leavengood
04 Logan, David					x	x		x		x	x	x	
09 Lockridge, James										x	x	x	
Loughridge, John	x	x	x	x	x	x	x		x	x	x	x	2-Loughrage 8Lawhr'
*03 Lockridge, Robert			x	x	x						x		
Lockridge, William	x	x	x	x		x	x		x	x	x	x	0/1-Loughridge
03 Long, Samuel			x	x	x	x		x	x	x	x	x	
Louderback, Andrew	x	x	x	x	x	x		x		x	x	x	9-Lauderback
Low, George	x	x		x	x	x		x		x	x	x	0-Lars 9-Lowe
08 Low, Isaac									x	x	x	x	
M													
10 Maddan, Susan											x		----see Mathers
10 Maffett, Henry											x	x	
*07 Maffett, Matthew								x		x		x	
03 Moffet, Thomas			x	x	x			x		x	x	x	5-Mofford 7Maffett
07 Maffett, William								x		x	x	x	
Man, John	x	x	x			x	x		x	x	x	x	
801 Man, Peter		x	x	x	x	x	x		x	x		x	
10 Manin, H.											x		----
10 Manin, Jacob											x		----
06 Mannens, Meredith							x		x	x	x	x	6-'er 9 Kenneth
06 Mannens, Samuel							x		x	x	x	x	6'er 8'on 9Mansire
10 Marell-----											x		----
Marsh, Thomas	x	x	x	x	x	x	x		x	x	x		
Marshall, Archibald	x	x	x	x	x	x	x		x		x		x	3-Alexander
Marshall, David	x	x	x							x	x	x	
08 Marshall, Hugh									x	x	x	x	
Marshall, Ralph	x	x		x	x	x					x		3-Realph
Marshall, Samuel	x		x	x	x	x		x		x	x		
03 Martin, James			x						x	x			
10 Martin, Michael											x		----(Mastin)
*02 Marten Nehemiah				x	x	x	x		x		x		x
*09 Masen, Benjamin									x		x		11-Mason
*Mason, Burgess	x	x	x	x	x	x		x	x		x		2-Mayson 9 Masen
06 Mathers, Gian							x		x	x	x	x	8-Garvin
08 Mathers, James									x		x	x	
Mathers, Samuel	x	x				x	x	x	x		x		

Person	18 00	01	02	03	04	05	06	07	08	09	10	11	
Mathers, William	x	x	x	x	x	x	x		x	x	x	x	3-Madders
*06 Maxwell, William							x		x	x		x	
10 Maynor, Jesse											x-----		
02 McCabe, Jossiah			x	x	x	x	x			x	x	x	
01 McCall, James		x	x	x	x	x			x	x	x	x	
09 McCall, John									x	x	x		
10 McChan, Daniel											x-----		
McCarty, David	x	x	x	x	x	x		x		x	x	x	
01 McCarty, Thomas		x	x	x	x	x		x		x	x	x	
09 McClain, Charles									x	x			10-McCain
McClannahan, James	x	x	x	x	x	x	x		x		x	x	2-McClanagen
McClannahan, Wm.	x		x	x	x	x			x	x	x	x	9-McClinagin
McClintock, Hugh	x	x	x	x	x	x	x		x	x	x	x	
McClintock, Joseph	x	x	x	x	x	x	x	x	x		x	x	2- McK 6-Clintock
*McClintock, Joseph, Jr.	x	x	x	x	x	x				x			
McClurgh, Joseph	x	x	x	x	x	x			x	x	x		
10 McConice, Christopher											x-----		
McCord, David	x	x	x	x	x	x		x		x	x	x	see Cord
03 McCord, John			x					x		x	x	x	
McCord, Michael	x	x	x	x	x	x		x		x	x	x	
McCord, William	x	x	x	x	x	x		x		x	x		
*McCord, William, Sr.	x	x	x	x						x			
*07 McCormick, Adam							x			x			
05 McCormick, Elizabeth						x	x		x	x	x	x	11-Widdow
*McCormach, James	x	x	x	x	x							x	
01 McCouns, Lawrenis		x								x			10-McCown, 'rence
06 McCoy, Daniel							x		x	x			
McCune, John	x	x	x	x	x	x	x		x	x	x	x	5-Sr.
McCune, Robert	x	x	x	x	x	x	x		x	x	x	x	
05 McCune, Robert, Jr.						x	x		x	x	x	x	
10 McDole, James											x-----		
10 McDole, William											x-----		
McDonal, Alexander	x	x	x	x	x	x	x	x	x	x	x	x	2-McDannal 6-Sr.
McDonald, Alexander	x		x		x	x			x	x			9-McDanald
McDonald, George	x	x	x	x		x	x		x	x	x	x	2-McDannal
09 McDanold, John									x	x			
McDonald, Joseph	x			x	x	x		x	x	x	x		
10 McDanald, Mary											x-----		
McDonald, Mordicay	x	x		x	x	x		x		x	x		
*04 McDowell, James						x		x		x		x	
01 McDowell, Mary		x		x		x				x			(10 no surname)

126

Person	18 00	01	02	03	04	05	06	07	08	09	10	11	Notes
McFarland, William	x	x	x	x	x	x		x		x	x	x	2-McFarling
01 McGinnis, William		x	x	x	x	x	x		x	x	x		
10 McGlolan, John										x			
10 McGlolan, John (10a)										x			(looks duplicated)
10 McGuire, John										x	x		
08 McIntire, Joseph									x	x	x		
*09 McLaughlin, John											x		x
03 McLease, William			x	x	x	x			x		x	x	4'Cleebe,5'Clees,8'Lees
McMahan, Robert	x	x	x		x	x	x		x	x	x	x	
10 McMahan, Robert (10a)										x----------			
*04 McMihell, John					x	x	x					x	5-McMichell
06 McMichel, Thomas							x			x	x	x	9McMihil
09 McNulty, James										x	x	x	11-McAnally
*09 McNulty, John										x		x	
McNulty, Joseph	x	x	x	x	x	x	x		x	x	x	x	2McInutty 6McAnulty
*09 McQuion, Lawrence										x		x	
10 Menach, Alexander										x	x		
10 Meredith, Absolum										x			
Metcalf, Eli	x	x	x	x	x	x		x		x	x	x	
Metcalf, Thomas	x	x	x	x	x	x		x			x	x	2-Matcalf
*Miller, Abraham	x	x		x				x		x		x	
*07 Miller, Abraham, Jr.								x		x		x	
09 Miller, James										x	x	x	
10 Mitchel, Ezekiel										x	x		
08 Moler, Isaac									x	x	x		
09 Monicle, Christopher										x	x	x	
04 Monigal, George					x	x		x			x	x	
02 Monical, Peter			x		x	x			x	x	x		4-Monigal
02 Moore, John			x	x		x			x		x		
Moore, Samuel	x	x	x	x		x	x		x		x	x	
08 Morgan, Agnes									x		x	x	
Morgan, Charles	x	x	x	x	x	x				x	x	x	
Morgan, Garret	x	x	x	x	x	x	x		x	x	x	x	2/3-Garrard 8Jared
*Morgan, Joseph	x	x	x	x	x	x					x		
10 Morris, Morris										x	x		
Morris, Thomas	x	x	x	x	x	x	x				x	x	
10 Mullin, Samuel										x	x		
10 Munson, Joel										x	x		11-Monson
Murphey, W. George	x	x	x	x	x	x	x		x	x	x		
05 Murphy, Zepheniah					x	x		x	x	x	x		
02 Myers, David	x					x		x	x	x	x		

Person	18 00	01	02	03	04	05	06	07	08	09	10	11	
*Myers, George	x	x	x	x	x	x	x		x	x		x	6-Miers
Myers, John	x	x	x	x	x	x	x		x	x	x	x	
*06 Miers, Lewis							x		x			x	8-Myers
08 Myers, Margaret									x	x	x	x	
N													
10 Neaves, Daniel											x	x	
08 Nelson, Moses									x		x	x	
10 Nesbet, John											x-----		
*Nesbet, Nathan	x	x	x	x	x	x	x					x	6-Nathaniel
Nesbet, Thomas	x	x	x		x	x	x		x		x	x	
10 Nesbet, Thomas (10a)											x-----		
Nickel, Robert	x	x	x	x	x	x	x		x		x	x	2-Nicholas
Newcum, Daniel	x	x	x	x					x				1-Nucum 3-Nukim
09 Nudigate, John										x	x	x	
Nudigate, William	x	x	x	x	x	x		x		x	x	x	
10 N-------, Yancy											x-----		
O													
10 Obadiah,---											x-----		
10 Ogdon, Mary											x-----		
10 Olanan, Susan											x-----		
Oliver, John	x	x	x	x	x	x		x			x	x	
10 Olliver, Thomas											x-----		
10 Orr, John											x-----		
10 Overby, Henry											x	x	
07 Overfield, Moses								x			x	x	
P													
09 Padget, Daniel										x	x	x	
Parks, James	x	x	x	x					x		x	x	
03 Parson, John				x	x	x	x				x	x	3-Person
10 Parter, James											x-----		
02 Patton, Stephen			x								x		
04 Pauley, John					x	x	x		x	x	x	x	9 Pawley
*04 Pauley, William					x	x	x		x			x	
Paxton, Robert	x	x	x			x	x				x	x	
01 Pendergrass, Edward		x	x	x	x	x	x		x		x	x	
10 Pecherer, Nancy											x-----		
Peyton, Samuel	x	x	x	x	x		x		x		x	x	
Peyton, Stephen	x	x		x	x	x	x		x		x	x	
06 Peyton, Stephen, Jr.							x		x		x	x	
Peyton, Thomas	x	x	x	x	x	x	x		x		x	x	
10 Phillip, John											x	x	10-(Donan)

Person	00	01	02	03	04	05	06	07	08	09	10	11	Notes
10 Phillips, Joshua											x-----		
Plew, Elias	x	x	x	x	x	x	x		x	x	x		1-Plue 3-Plough
Plew, Jeremiah	x	x	x	x	x	x	x		x	x	x	x	1-Plue 3 Plough
*Plew, Philip	x						x					x	
*03 Poe, William			x	x		x				x		x	
01 Potts, Frederick		x						x			x		
10 Pots, Samuel											x----		
Potts, William	x	x	x	x	x				x	x	x	x	
01 Powel, Charles		x	x	x	x	x	x		x		x	x	
04 Powel, George				x	x		x				x		
*08 Powel, Isaac									x			x	
05 Powel, Jeremiah					x	x			x		x	x	
04 Powel, John				x	x	x			x	x	x	x	
Powel, Thomas	x	x	x	x	x	x	x		x	x	x	x	
05 Powel, Thomas, Jr.						x			x		x	x	
10 Powel, William											x-------		10-Power
04 Powel, Zenis					x	x	x		x		x	x	
10 Prather, Ashford											x	x	
05 Prater, Jeremiah						x		x			x	x	7-Sr.
07 Prater, Jeremiah, Jr.								x			x	x	
Pritchet, William	x	x	x	x	x	x		x			x	x	1-Protchet 5-Pritchell
03 Pursley, Thomas			x	x	x						x	x	10-Purcell
02 Pursley, William	x		x	x		x	x				x	x	2-Purnal 5-Purnell

R

Person	00	01	02	03	04	05	06	07	08	09	10	11	Notes
09 Ramsey, Archibald										x	x	x	
*08(Randall), Richard									x	x		x	9-Rannals
*02 Rankin, Moses			x	x	x	x		x		x		x	
Ray, Francis, Sr.	x	x	x	x	x		x	x	x	x	x	x	4-Sr.
02 Reding, Eli			x								x	x	
03 Redding, William				x	x	x	x		x	x	x	x	4-Reading
10 Retzel, Peter											x	x	11-Retzatt
Reveal, Joseph	x	x	x	x	x	x	x		x	x	x	x	0/1-Reviel 10 Riveel
06 Reveal, Michael							x			x	x	x	
Reveal, Thomas	x			x	x	x	x		x	x	x	x	0/1-Reviel
*05 Richard, William						x			x			x	5-Richarts
Reily, John	x	x	x	x	x	x	x		x		x	x	2-Rily 3-Ryley
07 Ritche, Asy								x		x	x	x	9 Asaph 11Esau
Richey, Gilbert	x							x			x	x	
Richey, Isaac	x		x	x	x		x			x	x	x	7-Ritche
09 Ritchy, Noah										x	x	x	
Richey, Robert	x	x	x		x	x	x		x	x	x	x	

Person	1800	01	02	03	04	05	06	07	08	09	10	11	
06 Richee, Solomon							x				x	x	
06 Richee, William							x				x		
Roads, Becham	x	x	x	x	x	x	x		x		x	x	0/1-Rhoads
09 Rhodes, Silas										x	x	x	11-Roads
10 Roberts, John											x	x	
Roberts, Henly	x	x	x	x	x	x	x		x	x	x	x	2-Hely 3-Hanley
01 Roberts, Hezekiah		x	x	x	x	x			x	x	x		
01 Roberts, Neily		x		x	x	x					x		
Roberts, Thomas	x		x	x	x	x	x		x	x	x	x	
02 Robertson, Allexander			x	x	x		x		x		x	x	
10 Robertson, C.											x- - - - - - -		
10 Robertson, David											x- - - - - - -		
*Robertson, James	x	x	x	x	x		x		x	x		x	1-Robeson
*Robertson, Samuel	x	x	x	x	x	x	x		x	x		x	1-Robeson
09 Ross, Allexander									x	x	x		
10 Rozier, Adam											x- - - - - - -		
10 Runels, Michael											x- - - - - - -		
S													
10 Sadler, Edward											x	x	
Sadler, John	x	x	x	x	x	x	x		x	x	x	x	9-Sater
10 Sample, Mary											x		
*01 Sanders, Hezekiah		x	x	x	x	x						x	4-Sau
*Sanders, James	x		x	x	x	x			x			x	4-Saunders
*09 Sanderson, John										x		x	
10 Sanderson, Mary											x- - - - - - -		
06 Sanderson, Robert							x		x		x		
*09 Sater, John										x		x	
10 Savatier, William											x- - - - - - -		
06 Scott, Andrew							x		x	x	x	x	
Scott, John	x	x	x	x	x	x			x	x	x	x	2-Seat
Scott, Mathew	x	x	x	x	x	x		x	x	x	x		2-Seat
Scott, Thomas	x	x	x	x	x	x	x	x	x	x	x	x	2-Seat
Scott, Thomas (0a)	x	x		x	x				x	x	x	x	8-Jr.
09 Scott, Thomas, Sr.									x	x			
10 Selby, Isaac											x	x	
10 Shankfort, Agnes											x- - - - - - -		
09 Shankland, James									x	x			
Shankland, John	x	x	x	x	x	x	x		x	x	x	x	2-Shankling
08 Shannon, John									x	x	x		
06 Shannon, Margaret							x		x	x	x	x	
*01 Shannon, Samuel		x	x				x		x		x		

130

Person	18	00	01	02	03	04	05	06	07	08	09	10	11	
08 Sharp, John (T.)										x	x	x	x	9-Shaps
11 Short, George													x	
02 Sloop, Joseph				x	x	x	x		x		x	x	x	
10 Smalley, John												x	x	
09 Smith, Abrah											x	x	x	11-Absolum
03 Smith, David					x	x	x	x		x	x		x	
10 Smith, Gus											x----			
07 Smith, Hezekiah									x		x	x		
08 Smith, Hugh										x	x	x		
*05 Smith, James						x		x					x	
Smith, John	x	x						x		x	x	x	x	
*08 Smith, John (8a)										x			x	
06 Smith, Mitchel								x		x		x	x	
Smith, William	x	x			x	x	x		x		x	x	x	
*09 Snap, Daniel											x		x	
Snap, George	x	x		x	x	x	x		x			x	x	5-Sr.
*01 Snap, John		x			x	x	x		x	x			x	
Snap, Peter	x	x	x	x	x	x	x		x	x	x	x		
09 Snap, Samuel											x	x	x	
01 Spaw, Henry		x	x	x	x	x	x	x			x	x		3-Spaugh 4-Sporr
07 Spaw, Jacob									x		x	x	x	
*Standiford, Aquila	x	x	x	x	x	x				x			x	2-Equalay 9Quilly
01 Sandiford, George		x	x	x	x	x		x		x	x	x	x	2-St
09 Standeford, John											x		x	
07 Standiford, Sarah									x		x			
*08 Steals, James										x			x	8-Stears
*04 Steel, William						x	x			x			x	8-Stears
10 Stephenson, Eliza												x	x	11-Betsy
02 Stevenson, Joseph				x	x	x		x			x	x	x	
Stephenson, Robert	x	x		x	x			x			x	x		
09 Stephenson, Robert, Jr.											x	x	x	
Stephenson, Thomas	x	x	x	x	x	x			x		x	x	x	2-Stevenson
*Stephenson, William	x	x		x	x	x				x			x	
Stewart, Joseph	x	x	x	x	x	x		x		x	x	x		
06 Stewart, Mary							x			x		x	x	
Stewart, Williby('oughby)	x	x	x	x	x	x		x		x	x	x		3-Stuart
06 Stockwell, John							x		x	x	x	x		
02 Stogdel, James			x	x					x		x	x	x	7-Stogdale
03 Stogal, William				x					x		x	x	x	
Stoops, Phillip	x		x	x	x	x	x		x	x	x	x		
10 Surs, John											x----			

Person	18	00	01	02	03	04	05	06	07	08	09	10	11	
07 Swain, Nathan									x		x	x	x	
10 Swanson, John												x-----		
10 Swanson, John (10a)												x-----		
Swarts, James		x		x		x	x		x		x	x		
10 Swart, H.												x-----		
Sumet, Christian		x	x	x	x	x	x	x		x	x	x	x	3-Summit-Summersett
Sumet, George		x	x	x	x		x	x		x	x	x	x	3-Summit-Summersett
08 Summerfield, Richard										x	x	x	x	10 -'veal 11'sett
05 Sutton, Ebenzer						x	x		x		x			5-Shuttan
05 Sutton, John						x	x		x		x			5 Shuttan
T														
10 T----, Titus												x-----		
03 Taylor, George				x					x	x	x	x	x	
09 Taylor, George (9a)										x	x	x		
02 Taylor, John			x	x	x	x			x		x	x	x	2-Talor 11-Sr.
02 Tayler, Joshua			x	x	x	x	x			x	x	x		
03 Taylor, Nathaniel				x	x	x			x		x	x	x	
09 Taylor, Tapley										x	x	x		
Thomas, Edward		x	x	x	x	x	x	x		x	x	x	x	
Thompson, Alexander		x	x	x	x	x	x	x		x	x	x		
08 Thompson, Daniel										x	x	x	x	
*Thompson, Henry		x	x	x	x	x	x	x		x	x		x	1-Thomson 11-Sr.
*04 Thomson, H. James					x	x	x			x		x		
03 Thompson, James				x	x	x			x			x	x	5-Sr.
06 Thompson, Sarah							x			x	x	x		
Thompson, William		x	x		x	x	x	x		x	x	x	x	
10 Thornton, Anthony											x	x		
10 Throckmorton, Ari											x	x		11-Ariss
02 Throckmorton, John			x	x	x	x		x		x	x	x	x	7/9-Thogmorton
Throckmorton, Thomas		x	x	x	x	x	x		x	x	x	x	x	0-listed Morton
01 Throckmorton, Th.,Jr.			x		x	x	x		x	x	x	x		
10 Tomkins, K.												x		10(Kinsnit ?)
10 Trulove, Will C.												x	x	
V														
01 Vanhook, Abner			x		x	x	x		x		x	x		
01 Vanhook, Archiles			x		x	x	x		x		x	x		4-Archibald 7 'helaus
03 Vanhook, Samuel				x		x		x		x	x			
06 Vanskike, Hezekiah							x		x	x	x	x		
10 Vaugh, Jacob												x-----		
10 Vaugh, Jacob (10a)												x-----		
Vaughn, Thomas		x	x	x	x	x	x	x		x	x	x	x	2-Vaun -3 Vawn

132

Person	18 00	01	02	03	04	05	06	07	08	09	10	11	
Vennoy, Francis	x	x	x	x	x	x					x	x	10-Bernoy
04 Verden, Hugh				x	x			x		x	x	x	7-Vurden
W													
Waggoner, Christian	x	x	x	x	x	x			x		x	x	5-Christopher
Waggoner, John	x	x	x	x	x	x		x		x	x	x	
10 Wates, Charles										x--------			
Waits, John	x	x		x	x	x		x			x		4/5-Wales 7Wiets
Wallace, William	x	x	x	x	x	x		x		x	x	x	2-Wallis
10 Warren, Isaac											x	x	11-Warrant
Watson, James	x	x	x	x	x	x		x		x	x	x	
03 Watson, James, Jr.			x	x	x			x		x	x		
*07 Waugh, Jacob								x		x		x	
*Waugh, Samuel (M.)	x	x	x	x	x	x	x		x			x	
*03 Web, Charles			x		x					x		x	11-Webb
*06 Webster, Nathan							x					x	11-Nathaniel
03 Wells, Aaron			x			x					x	x	Wells/Wills
10 Wills, Charles										x--------			
10 Wills, David										x--------			
Wills, John	x	x	x	x			x		x	x	x	x	Wills/Wells
10 Wells, Nathan											x	x	
West, Amos	x	x	x	x	x	x	x		x	x	x	x	
*03 West, Eli			x		x	x				x		x	9-Elijah
09 West, John									x	x	x		
09 West, John (9a)									x	x			
*West, Isaac	x	x	x	x	x	x	x		x	x		x	
09 West, Philip										x	x	x	
West, Thomas	x		x	x	x	x		x		x	x	x	
10 West, Thomas (10a)										x--------			
Wheeler, William	x	x		x		x	x		x		x	x	
09 Whitaker, James										x	x	x	
05 White, John					x	x		x			x	x	
09 Whitely, David										x	x	x	10-Daniel
09 Whitly, William										x	x	x	
Wiggons, John	x	x	x	x	x	x		x		x	x	x	2-Wigon
07 Wiggons, William								x		x	x	x	9-Wiggins
05 Wiley, Hugh						x			x	x	x	x	
Wiley, John	x		x		x	x	x		x		x	x	2-Wile 6-Sr.
06 Wiley, John, Jr.							x		x	x	x	x	
Wiley, Samuel	x			x	x	x	x		x	x	x	x	
*04 Wiley, William					x	x	x		x	x		x	
03 Williamson, John				x	x	x					x	x	

Person	1800	01	02	03	04	05	06	07	08	09	10	11	
Williams, John	x	x	x	x	x	x	x		x	x	x	x	
09 Williams, William										x	x	x	
Wilson, Benjamin	x	x	x	x	x		x			x	x	x	1-Willon
*08 Wilson, Charles									x	x		x	
09 Wilson, Isaac										x	x	x	
05 Wilson, James					x		x			x	x		
10 Wilson, James (10a)										x--------			
10 Wilson, Jane										x--------			
*06 Wilson, John						x						x	
10 Woolen, Leonard										x	x		
09 Woolens, William									x	x	x		
10 Wood, Hilkiah										x	x		
Y													
04 Yates, Andrew				x					x	x	x	x	
04 Yates, William				x						x			
03 Young, Allexander			x		x					x	x	x	
Young, Jacob	x			x	x	x	x		x	x	x	x	

LOCATING SURNAMES

How do you locate surnames? Why do you compare spellings?

These eleven years of tax lists should prove to anyone that any surname can be spelled numerous ways or at least that several modern researchers can view old hand writing in different ways. Many times, I have mistaken "Smith" for some other name.
1. Many clerks (and their assistants) had little education.
2. 1800 was a period before standard spellings had been accepted.
3. Penmanship was not standard. For example the ss which looked like f.
4. Ink was usually homemade and faded over the years.
5. Books were damaged by water, bookworms or man.

So, what can a researcher do to insure no relatives are overlooked?

1. Read original records until you can understand them.
2. When using microfilm, see if originals exist.
3. If county clerks change, spend time viewing the new clerk's entries.
4. Compare - compare - compare. Use as many county records as you can, because each court kept records with a different clerk.

The preceeding pages of tax lists were collected by the sherriff's office.
Following are the indexes to the deed books which were kept by the county clerk.

A third list would be those taken by the census enumerator.

INDEXES TO FIRST THREE DEEDS BOOKS

NICHOLAS COUNTY,

KENTUCKY

Copied from loose index pages which are inserted in each deed book.

Court House, Carlisle, Kentucky

INDEX TO NICHOLAS COUNTY, KENTUCKY
DEED BOOK   A&B 1801-1808

Tax books and deed books compliment each other and allow name verification.
These indexes are not attached to the deed books, but a series of loose pages
(single folded sheets of paper with writing on both sides and kept with book).
They are in bad shape and pages are separated from each other.
This copy is an effort to preserve the index.
* entries without reciprical entry

++   Note: There are actually 2 indexes for BOOK A & B, but neither is labeled A or B
         Some entries (in one book only) are numbered and then lettered.
         Entries will be labeled 1) or 2) and two lists will be made.

A			Boggas from same	283(1
Anderson to Fowler	72(1		Baker from Eslick	308(1
Adrey Jr. to Kincart	306(1		Buntin from Fowler	297(1
same to Mathers	162(1		Breckinridge from Jones	351(1
Arnold from Drake	121(1		Ballingal form Kilgore	314(1
B			Barlow from Richey	20(1
*Buckner to Standeford B&S	32(1		Buchanan from Thornton	107(1
* same to Throckmorton	37(1		C	
*Barlow to Barlow	40(1		C.C. Justices to Buchanan	2(1
Byers to Price	44(1		*Caldwell to Caldwell	16(1
*Buckner to Throckmorton	78(1		Cook to Barlow	17(1
* same to same	79(1		same to Groghegan	22(1
* same to Buckner's deed gift	81(1		same to Snap	97(1
Buchanan to Taylor	149(1		same to Lilly	99(1
Brooks art. of freedom	228(1		*C.C. Justices to McClintock 113(1	
Brown to McGinnis	264(1		* same to Culp	120(1
same to Thomas	267(1		Commissioners to McDowell 141(1	
*Ballingal to McCormick	309(1		same to Wilson	144(1
*Beaford to Bedinger	346(1		same to Sanders	157(1
Buchanan from C.C. Justices	2(1		*same to Williams	198(1
Barlow from Cook	17(1		Combs & US to Baxter	210(1
Baxter from (Comtes & uk)	210(1		*C.C. Justices to McClintock 212(1	
Buchanan from Drake	182(1		* same to Jones	216(1
Baker from Depaw	201(1		* same to Caldwell	229(1
Buchanan from Drake	242(1		* same to Vaughan	231(1

INDEX TO DEED BOOK A-B

INDEX TO DEED BOOK A-B

G

Groghegan to Murphey	25(1
same to Richey	28(1
same to Waggoner	54(1
same to H. Githens	92(1
Grant & Others to Kimbrough	124(1
Groghegan to Standiford	232(1
same to same	251(1
Galbreath to Galbreath	364(1
Groghegan from Cook	22(1
Githens, H. from Groghegan	92(1
*Githens, J. from same	94(1
Galbreath from Galbreath	364(1
Groghegan from Hawes	75(1
Gray from Irvin	322(1
Gray & Alison from Irvin	328(1
Galbreath from Marshall	104(1
Gray from McKinsey	354(1
Griffin from Young	217(1

H

Harrison to Caughey, lease	42(1
same to Campbell, LA	58(1
Hawes to Groghegan	75(1
*Harrison, Titus-Cert.of Freedom	89(1
Henry to Kenton	115(1
same to Clarke	146(1
*Harrison & Stubbs (M.C.)	166(1
Hall & Co. to Marshall	173(1
same to Frazier	175(1
Henderson to Thomson	196(1
Henry to Clarke	254(1
same to Prichard	255(1
*Hinkson from Allison	358(1
*Henry from Clarke	252(1
Harney from Eslick	171(1
Hall from Fowler	69(1
same from same	293(1
Hedrick from Shillinger P.A.	119(1
Hawkins from Standiford	138(1
Hildreth from Thornton	52(1

Henderson from Thompson	158(1
same from same	193(1

I

Irvin to Smith	277(1
same to Irvin	279(1
Irvin to Gray	322(1
same to Gray & Allison	328(1
Irvin from Irvin	279(1
Irvin from Johnson	318(1

J

*Jones to Wigglesworth	207(1
*Johnston to Johnston	282(1
Johnston to Irvin	318(1
Jones to Breckinridge	351(1
Johnson from Drake	275(1
Justice, C.C. from Ellis	288(1
Johnson from Eslick	310(1
Johnson from Johnson	282(1
Jackson from Kenton	280(1
Jones from Thornton	49(1
Jones from Young	302(1

K

Kenton Reps. to Kenton	84(1
same to Combs	87(1
Kenton to Duncan	117(1
Kimbrough to Kimbro	185(1
Kenton to Standiford	203(1
same to Thorockmorton	223(1
same to Jackson	280(1
Kincart to Ardery, Jr.	306(1
Kilgour to Ballingal	314(1
Kenton to Duncan	347(1
Kimbrough from Grant	124(1
Kenton from Harny (Henry)	115(1
Kenton from Kenton's Rep.	84(1
Kimbrough from Kimbrough	185(1
Kenton from Monroe	238(1
Kimbrough from Young	129(1
same from same	304(1

INDEX TO DEED BOOK A-B

L		N	
*Lilly & ux to Kimbrough	183(1	Nicholas Comm. to McDowell	141(1
Lilly from Cook	99(1	same to Wilson	144(1
M		Newdigate from Thornton	35(1
Marshall to Ellis	101(1	**O**	
same to Galbreath	104(1	Olliver to Parks	245(1
*McShain to Wait agt.	106(1	Olliver from Sordon	311(1
*Marshall to Waugh & Archer	132(1	**P**	
Mitchell to Wood	136(1	Peers to Taylor	324(1
McDowell to Peyton	155(1	Parks to Dowain	344(1
Mathers to Ardery	162(1	Price from Byers	44(1
Metcalf to Davis	208(1	Potts from Fowler	67(1
Monroe's Comm. to Kenton	238(1	Pullin from Fearman	315(1
Marney to Drummons	259(1	Prichard from Henry	255(1
Marshall to McDonald	269(1	Peyton from McDowell	155(1
Man to Man	331(1	Parks from Oliver	245(1
same to same	333(1	Peyton from Wilson	164(1
same to same	335(1	**R**	
McKinsey to Gray	354(1	*Ragsdale to Standiford B & S	1(1
McKinsey to Drake	355(1	Richey to Barlow	20(1
Marshall to Marshall	366(1	Roberts from Fowler	188(1
*Morgan from Arnold	290(1	same from same	190(1
McGinnis from Brown	264(1	Richey from Groghegan	28(1
McCormick from Ballingal	309(1	**S**	
McDowell from Co. Comm.	141(1	Shillinger to Hedrick - PA	119(1
Mann from Ellis	257(1	Standiford to Hawkinis	138(1
McDonald from same	260(1	* same to Williams	214(1
McAnulty from Fowler	11(1	Sheriff to Metcalf	235(1
McCoy from same	33(1	Sporr to Wiggins	316(1
Murphey from Groghegan	25(1	Sordon to Olliver	337(1
Marshall from Hall & Co.	173(1	Snap from Cook	97(1
McDonald from Marshall	269(1	Sanders from Comm.	157(1
Mann from Mann	331(1	Shaw from Claytor	262(1
same from same	333(1	Standiford from Drake	226(1
same from same	335(1	Sanders from Fowler	9(1
Marshall from Marshall	366(1	Stephenson from same	63(1
Metcalf from sheriff	235(1	Standiford from Grohegan	232(1
McDowell from Wilson	153(1	same from same	251(1
Mann from Waggoner	179(1	Smith from Irvin	277(1

INDEX DEED BOOK A-B

INDEX #2 DEED BOOK A-B
All entries following a(book) letter change are apparently of that letter.
* Indicates entry without reciprical entry.

Artt to Artt	69B(2	Boulder from Enlow	87B(2
Allison to Deea	72 (2	Bedinger & Vaughan	
*Anderson to Anderson	105 & 259(2	from Finley	85A(2
* same to same	107 (2	Ballingal from Gamble	175B(2
Allison to Gray	137 (2	Bedinger from Hughes	3A(2
Anderson to Mitchell	155 (2	same from same	4A(2
* same to Gray	157 (2	same from Hite	42B(2
Allison to Taylor	173 (2	Bodley from Hall	142B(2
Anderson to Bontain	193 (2	Barlettt from Hughes	183B(2
Anderson from Fowler	52A(2	Ballingal from Jones	125B(2
*Alexander from Ferguson	68B(2	Buchanan from Kenton	10B(2
Allison from Gray	39B(2	Baker from Kimbrough	54B(2
Asberry from Kenton	47B(2	Bedinger from Marshall	24A(2
Anderson from Metcalf	18A(2	same from same	28A(2
same from Powell	121B(2	Beard fromMartin	88A(2
same from Roberts' cond.	109B(2	same from Rineholdt	137A(2
Art from Rineholdt	141A(2	Bartlett from Ragsdale	119B(2
B		Burns from Stoops	100A(2
Buckner to Saunders	59 (2	Bodley from Purviance	164B(2
same to Martin	62 (2	C	
same to Welch	64 (2	Caldwell to Gray	26B(2
same to Wallace	67 (2	Caughey to Ballingal	56-208(2
same to Rankins	70 (2	*C.C. Justices to Waugh	57 (2
same to Wiggins	72 (2	* same to Tompking	58 (2
Ballingal to King	83 (2	* same to Daughty	60 (2
Boyd to Martin	90 (2	* same to Whitaker	76 (2
Baker to Hendirx	105 (2	Chinn to Bennett	95 (2
same to Feeback	115 (2	*C.C. Justice to Stockwell	163 (2
Berry to West	1B(2	*Caldwell to Yates	185 (2
Buckner to Groghegan	61B(2	same to Murphy	188 (2
same to Jones	63B(2	*C.C.Justices to Whitesell	195 (2
*Ballingal to Brown	161B(2	Cowan to Howard	197 (2
Bartlett from Marshall	31A(2	Caldwell from Dawson	169B(2
Buntin from Anderson	193B(2	Carter from Ellis	8A(2
Ballingal from Caughey	56B(2	same from same	50A(2
Bennett from Chinn	95B(2	Caldwell from Fowler 151A(2	

INDEX #2 DEED BOOK A-B

Campbell from same	51B(2		Fearman from Ellis	5A(2
Clay from Hite	38A(2		Foster from Hall	20A(2
Chaney from Rawling's Com.	120A(2		Frazier from McConnico	159B(2
D			Fielder from Ragsdale	199B(2
Drake to Rankins	43B(2		**G**	
Deea to Throckmorton	74 (2		Glascock to Martin	1 (2
Dix & Walker to Jones	148 (2		Gray & ux to Throckmorton	37B(2
Dawson & ux to Caldwell	169 (2		same to Allison	39 (2
Dea from Allison	72B(2		same to Overby	139 (2
Dailey from Henry	83B(2		Gamble to Ballingal	175 (2
Drake from Kenton	9B(2		Gray from Allison	137B(2
Dowden from same	34B(2		Groghegan from Buckner	61B(2
Duzan from Mosely	132B(2		Gray from Caldwell	26B(2
Dowden from Overfield	125A(2		Glascock from Kenton	10A(2
same from same	127A(2		Gamble from Marshall	122A(2
E			**H**	
Ellis to Fearman	5 (2		Hughes to Bedinger	3 (2
same to Carter	8 (2		same to same	4 (2
same to same	50 (2		Harrison to Scott	13 (2
Easlick to Snap	80B(2		Hall to Foster	20 (2
Enlows to Boulden	87 (2		* same to same	21 (2
Eslick to Hamilton	124 (2		Hite to Clay	38 (2
Eslick from Mann	149A(2		same to Bedinger	42 (2
Evans from Stephenson	78A(2		Hall to Powell x21Bx	173 (2
Eaton from Taylor	144B(2		*Hall to Hall x27x	179 (2
Enlow from Wilson	85B(2		* same to same x29x	181 (2
*Estes from Young	118B(2		*Hendrix to Harney	70 (2
F			Henry to Daley	83 (2
Fowler to Caldwell	15 (2		Hall to Bodley x142x	294 (2
same to Anderson	52 (2		Harney to Ritchey	168 (2
same to Paugh	56 (2		Hughes to Bartlett	183 (2
Finley to Bedinger&Vaughan	85 (2		Hendrix from Baker	105A(2
Fendall & ux to Saunderson	92 (2		Howard from Cowan	197B(2
*Fowler to Thomson	45B(2		Hamilton from Eslick	124B(2
same to Campbell	51 (2		Herbert from Rineholdt	135A(2
same to Stephenson	53 (2		Honicle from same	139A(2
*Ferguson to Stephenson	68 (2		Howard from same	147A(2
Fowler to Riddle	130 (2		**I**	
same to Riley	152 (2		Irvin to Wiggins	6B(2
Feeback from Baker	115A(2		same to Ragsdale	65 (2

INDEX #2 DEED BOOK A-B

INDEX #2 DEED BOOK A-B

INDEX FOR NICHOLAS COUNTY
DEED BOOK C

Note: Not in cronological order . Should be if entries were made every day.
A few names have been returned to the correct alphabetical section.
* No reciprical entry.

INDEX TO DEED BOOK C

INDEX TO DEED BOOK C

INDEX TO DEED BOOK C

INDEX TO DEED BOOK C

INDEX TO DEED BOOK 3

INDEX TO DEED BOOK 3

NOTE: Spellings vary between entries and between reciprical entries

CONNECTIONS   While working with the Nicholas County Stray Books, I discovered a "connection" between Nicholas County and Cabell County, VA/WV. This "connection" occuried because an early surveyor (John P. Duvall) left many thousands of acres in western Virginia to his son who became a Nicholas County clerk and sold that Cabell land to people in Nicholas County.

These tax records show a "connection" between Nicholas County and the first settlers of eastern Tennessee and the soldiers of King's Mountain. There are too many similar surnames from both areas not to be connected. How could this happen? Remember, Nicholas County is a pass-through area along the main route from Cumberland Gap to the Ohio River now US 68.

NICHOLAS COUNTY SURNAMES IN WASHINGTON COUNTY, TENNESSEE

Source: *The Overmountain Men*
*uncommon names   Most would be sons, but not all.

Washington County, Tennessee Taxables 1778-1801

Allison	Edward	*Matlock	*Smart
Arnold	Davis	McCormick	Smith
Atkins	Drake	Martin	Taylor
Bayley	Duncan	McCartney	Thompson
Blackburn	*Easley	McMahan	Thornton
Blair	Fowler	Miller	Vance
Bradley	Griffith	Mitchell	Walton
Brown	Hamilton	Morgan	Ward
Buchanan	Hawkins	Moore	Weaver
Bunton	Henry	*Neave	Webb
Campbell	Hill	Randel	Wheeler
Carter	Hoffman	Rawlings	White
Casedy	Howard	Reding	Williams
Clark	Hughes	Riley	Wilson
Conway	Johnson	*Ritchie	Woods
Cooper	Jones	Roberts	Wray(Ray)
Cox	Kelly	Robertson	
Crawford	Kenedy	Scott	

SURNAMES FROM NICHOLAS COUNTY AND
GREENE COUNTY, TENNESSEE TAXABLES 1783
Source: *The Overmountain Men*

Allison	Eaton	Martin	Roberts
Alexander	Evans	McCall	Robertson
Anderson	Galbrath	McCartney	Sample
Armstrong	Gillispie	McClung	Scott
Barnett	Greene	McDowell	Steel
Beard	Hardin	McFarland	Stephenson
Borden	Hamilton	McFerrin	Stewart
Boyd	Hawkins	Miller	Stockton
Brown	Henry	Mitchell	Tate
Byram	Hill	Moore	Taylor
Cameron	Houston	Morgan	Thomas
Campbell	Howard	Morris	Thompson
Carter	Huffman	Mulholland	Wallace
Conway	Hughes	Murphy	Ward
Cooper	Johnson	Parks	Webb
Cowan	Jones	Phillips	Wells
Cox	Kelly	Prather	West
Craig	Kennedy	Price	Williams
Davis	Kilgore	Rankin	Wills
Dotson	King	Rawlings	Wilson
Doherty	Leeper	Ray	Wood
Duncan	Livingston	Reed	
Duval	Long	Richey	

SURNAMES FROM NICHOLAS COUNTY AND
KING'S MOUNTAIN REVOLUTIONARY BATTLE

Source: *The Overmountain Men*

Change some letters and several more names could be added

Adams	Daugherty	Lilies	Rhea(Ray)
Alexander	Davidson	Livingston	*Ritchie
Allen	Davis	Logan	Roberts
Allison	Doherty	Long	Robinson
Baker	Enlow	Lyon	Ross
Bartlett	Evans	Martin	Sample
Barnett	Foster	Marshall	Scott
Barnes	Fowler	Maxwell	Shannon
Berry	Fry	McCarthy	Sharp
Blackburn	Gamble	McCormick	Smart
Blair	Gillispie	McCoy	Smith
Bowen	*Galbreath	McDonald	Steel
Boyd	Graham	McDowell	Stevenson
Brooks	Gray	*McFarland	Stewart
Brown	Green	*McFerrin	*Stinson
Buchanan	Griffith	*Metcalf	Stockwell
Buckner	Hannah	Miller	Taylor
Burns	Harrison	Mitchel	Tate
Caldwell	Henderson	*Moffett	Thomas
Campbell	Henry	Monroe	Thompson
Carns	Hill	Morgan	Vance
*Caruthers	Houston	Murphy	*Vanhook
Carter	Hughes	Newman	Wallace
Casey	Hunter	Palmer	Walton
Clark	Ingle	Parks	Ward
Collins	Jenkins	Patton	Watson
Cooper	Jennings	*Pendergrass	Webb
Cosby	Johnson	Phillips	Wells
*Cowan	Kelly	Porter	White
*Coulter	Kennedy	Powel	Williams
Cox	Keys	*Prather	Wilson
Craig	Kilgore	Price	Wiley
Crawford	King	Rankin	Yates
Dalton	*Leeper	Rawlings	Young
	Leonard	Reed	

	Approximate	Per Cent
SURNAMES IN NICHOLAS COUNTY 1800-1811	1500	
SURNAMES WASHINGTON TO NICHOLAS	70	4.6%
SURNAMES GREENE TO NICHOLAS	90	6%
SURNAMES AT KINGS MOUNTAIN	136	9%

INDEX

Binns 35,55

Bishop, Teril 48

Black 2,16

Black, Richard 2

Blackburn, Julius H. 48

Blackburn, William 2,16

Blair, Alexander 2,16,47

Blout, Reding

Boatman, Henry 1,15,48

Boatman, William 15

Bodly 29,30,38,43,45

Boggess, Thomas 30,49

Bolard 8

Bolen, William 2,16

Boles, William 31,48

Boon, Abner 2,16

Boon, Jacob 2

Bosby, William 16

Boyd, John 2,16,48

Boyd, William 2,16

Bowen, William 1,31,48

Boyle, John 49

Bradley, David 49

Bradley, Robert 29,49

Bradshaw, David 31

Bradshaw, William 47

Brady, Elisha 30

Brady, George 30

Branon, Thomas 30

Brenton, James 48

Bright, Harrison 16

Brinson, Jonathan 30,49

Brinson, Thomas 2,16

Brinson, Thomas, Jr. 49

Brinson, Thomas Sr. 49

Brinton 30

Brookin, Robert 49

Brooks, Susanna 30

Brooks, Zachariah 48

Brown, Alexander 30,48

Brown, David 15

Brown, Ja. 31

Brown, James 1,15,29,30

Brown, John 2,16,29,30,31, 48,49

Brown, Jursey 49

Brown, Parker 48

Brown, William 48

Bryam, August 31

Buchannan, James 2,16

Buchannan, Pheobe 30,49

Buckler, Robert 30,49

Buckner 49

Buckner, Henry 49

Buckner, James 30

Buckner, Phillip 2

Buckner, Robert 2,16

Buckner, Samuel 30

Bullard 57

Buntin, Andrew 30

Buntin, Andrew 31

Bunton, Andrew 47

Bunton, James 47

Bunton, William 48

Burden, Benjamin 16

Burden, James 2,16

Burden, John 2,16,49

Burnet, William 48

Burns, Mathew

Burris, James 48

Burris, John 48,49

Burwell, Ephraim 2

Busby, Archibald 30,48

Busby, Mathew 48

Busby, William 30,48

Byers, David 1,15,48

Byers, John 48

Byram. Augustin 48

Byram, Valentine 48

Cack, David 31

Caha, John 31

Caldwell, Alexander, 3,17,51

Caldwell, David 3,17,32

Caldwell, David, Jr. 51

Caldwell, David, Sr. 51

Caldwell, Robert 16,17,32,51

Caldwell, Robert, Jr. 3,51

Caldwell, Robert, Sr. 51

Caldwell, Thomas 32,50

Caldwell, Walter 32

Caldwell, William 3,17

Caldwell, William, Jr. 51

Caldwell, William, Sr. 51

Caly, Thomas 50

Cameron, John 3,17

Cameron, Samuel 17,50

Campbell, Daniel 51

Campbell, David 3,17

Campbell, James 3,17, 32,51

Campbell, John 50

Campbell, Jonas 50

Campbell, Jossiah 3,16

Campbell, Robert 51

Campbell, William 2,3,17

Campble/Campbell

Canady 42

Canady, Robert 32

Carbough, Jacob 3,17

Carnahan, James 32

Carnahan, James M. 32

Carnahan, James, Jr. 51

Carnahan, James, Sr. 51

Carnahan, Robert 32,51

Carnes, Adam 50

Carothers, Thomas 3,17,31,50

Carpoell, Edward P. 16

Carrothers, Gabriel 50

Carter, Daniel 31,49

Carter, Jonathan 17,32

Carthers, Thomas 31

Carver 3

Casady, James 32

Casey, James 3,50

Casey, John 50

Cassabaugh, Ester 31

Cassady 36,40,44

While compiling the
11 years of tax entries,
several changes were
made from the original
interpertations. I have
choosen to retain the index
as first read so the reader
can understand how easy
it is to transpose letters.
a=o e=i e=c t=l r=s s=n
k=h ss=f b=h x=nn n=m
almost every letter.
S=L=T=F R=N=K etc.
Having an alphabetical
list helps only so far.

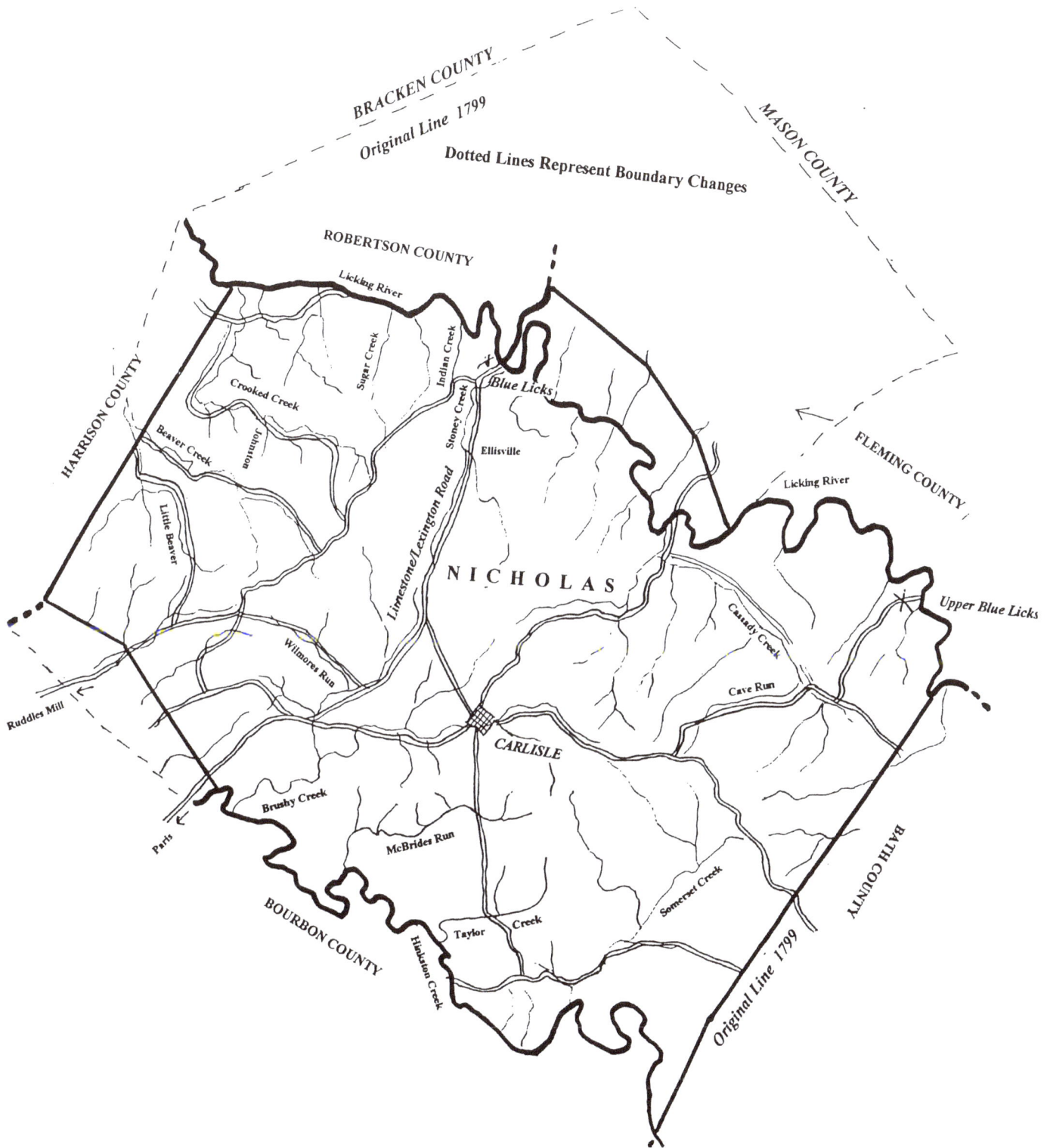

BRACKEN COUNTY

Original Line 1799

MASON COUNTY

Dotted Lines Represent Boundary Changes

ROBERTSON COUNTY

Licking River

HARRISON COUNTY

Sugar Creek

Crooked Creek

Indian Creek

Stoney Creek

Blue Licks

Beaver Creek

Johnston

Ellisville

Little Beaver

FLEMING COUNTY

Licking River

N I C H O L A S

Limestone/Lexington Road

Cassady Creek

Upper Blue Licks

Wilmores Run

Cave Run

Ruddles Mill

CARLISLE

Brushy Creek

Paris

McBrides Run

Somerset Creek

BATH COUNTY

BOURBON COUNTY

Taylor   Creek

Hinkston Creek

Original Line 1799

NICHOLAS COUNTY, KENTUCKY
Since 1799, Nicholas has lost almost 1/3 its original territory.

ABOUT THE AUTHOR

CARRIE ELDRIDGE is a product of Appalachia with deep roots in Ohio, West Virginia, Kentucky, and Tennessee. Her life-long interest in history and family has lead her to a bachelor's degree in secondary education, emphasizing Social Studies and Music, followed by a master's degree in historical geography emphasizing maps and remote sensing. These degrees were earned from Marshall University in Huntington, West Virginia where she volunteers in the Special Collection Department of Morrow Library and teaches Geography classes as an adjunct professor after many years as a classroom teacher.

For the last twenty-five years, she has abstracted and compiled local documents in West Virginia, Kentucky and Ohio, acted to preserve county records, and created maps to display geographical and genealogical information. Mrs. Eldridge has published thirty compiled court records and ten volumes of local history, including ten original maps. A series of pioneer migration atlases and a regional study on slave manumissions have brought nationwide recognition of her work.

The President of ELDERKIN, Mrs. Eldridge, acts as a local history consultant for numerous groups and university classes. She has created a brochure of historical cemetery sites for the Cabell County Landmark Society and speaks at local, regional and national genealogical events. Currently, an adjunct teacher of Geography at Marshall University and Shawnee State University, she is also involved in West Virginia records preservation and is assisting in the creation of an underground railroad society for West Virginia. Carrie Eldridge has been honored by Who's Who of the Midwest, by Who's Who of American Women, and by the Special Collections Department of Marshall University's Morrow Library.

www.ingramcontent.com/pod-product-compliance
Lightning Source LLC
Chambersburg PA
CBHW081505200326

41518CB00015B/2380